$\mathscr{A}$

BOSTON HARBOR ISLANDS
ADVENTURE

Ye Sqvare Partie
consisteth of:
ye Avtocrat
ye Aristocrat
ye Acrobat
and ye Scribe

Ye sqvare partie of ye Merrie Trippers—

Ye Avtocrat saith:
"Let vs seek the Sea-side, there
To wander idly as we list."

A

BOSTON HARBOR ISLANDS
ADVENTURE

THE GREAT BREWSTER JOURNAL *of* 1891

STEPHANIE SCHOROW
and the Friends of the Boston Harbor Islands

THE
History
PRESS

Published by The History Press
Charleston, SC
www.historypress.com

Front cover: A photo of a woman identified in the Great Brewster journal as "Ye Aristocrat" shows her at the end of the sandspit formed at low tide from Great Brewster Island. Fort Warren on Georges Island is in the background. *Frontispiece*: A self-portrait of the four "Merrie Trippers" who spent two weeks on Great Brewster Island in 1891.

First published 2023

Manufactured in the United States

ISBN 9781467151689

Library of Congress Control Number: 2022951508

CONTENTS

ACKNOWLEDGEMENTS

This book would not have been possible without the help of many people and institutions throughout New England. We must first thank Diana Carey and the staff of the Schlesinger Library of the Harvard Radcliffe Institute and Harvard professor John Stilgoe for their support of this project. We also have to thank Marta Crilly, archivist, City of Boston Archives; Daryl A. Forgione, regional engineer and project manager for the rehabilitation of Great Brewster Island for the Department of Conservation and Recreation; Lieutenant Alex Hall, of the Boston Harbor Islands State Park; and Jeremy D'Entremont, author and lighthouse expert. For their assistance with information on the photographs, we would like to thank Martha Cooper, author and collector of early Kodak advertising; Elizabeth Bischof, director of Osher Map Library, University of Southern Maine; Dan Colucci, collector and founder of the Internet Directory of Camera Collectors; Todd Gustavson, curator of technology, the George Eastman Museum; Kevin Johnson, photo archivist, Penobscot Marine Museum; Donna Russo, library and archive specialist, Historic New England; and Ann Sindelar, librarian, Cleveland History Center, Western Reserve Historical Society. We are also grateful to Kate Rivera and Karol Bartlett for their insights and support and to other members of the board of the Friends of the Boston Harbor Islands for approving this project.

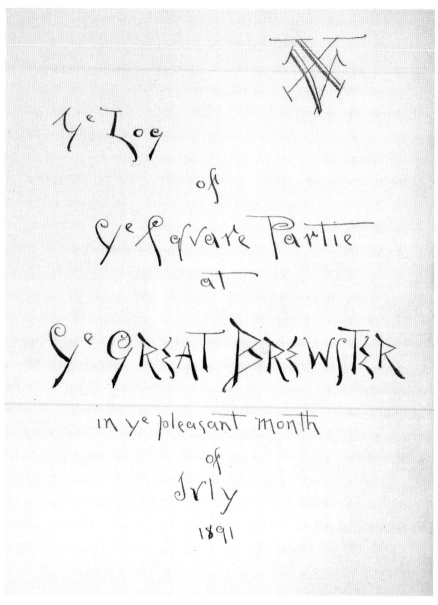

Ye Log of Ye Square Partie at Ye Great Brewster in ye pleasant month of July 1891

The women who visited Great Brewster Island adopted a kind of faux seaworthy language for their journal, adding to the impression that their trip was a sojourn to a place outside their normal lives. The XV logo of their women's club is drawn in the upper right side.

INTRODUCTION

My dream is of an island-place
Which distant seas keep lonely,
A little island on whose face
The stars are watchers only...
—*From "An Island" by Elizabeth Barrett Browning*

On a hot morning in July 1891, four women from Lowell, Massachusetts, gathered at a busy wharf in Boston, preparing to sail to a remote island in Boston Harbor. They were about to shed their identities as proper late nineteenth-century wives, mothers and dutiful daughters to become their most authentic selves, an almost radical act for an era in which women lacked even the basic right to vote. For the next seventeen days, they would rough it on Great Brewster Island, a nineteen-acre island on the far edges of the harbor, relishing both the solitude of an island escape and the companionship of dear friends.

They walked the rocky shore, read for hours—often out loud to one another—wrote letters and talked late into the evening. They took photos with the newly developed Kodak snapshot camera and painted exquisite watercolors of landscapes and flora. They answered only to one another and relied on their skills at gathering wood for their fire and for cooking delectable meals from their supplies. When they finally boarded a sailboat to take them home, they spoke of bidding "farewell to our enchanted Isle, so difficult to reach and so hard to leave," as if Great Brewster were a kind of Avalon, a mystical place not of this world.

It is only by chance that we know about these women and their adventure.

In the mid-1990s, John R. Stilgoe, the Robert and Lois Orchard Professor in the History of Landscape at the Visual and Environmental Studies Department of Harvard University, was riding his bike on Cape Ann, a popular seacoast area north of Boston. He stopped to change a tire and wandered into a nearby used bookstore. There, he almost immediately saw a curious book with a worn brown cover near the sales counter. He began to leaf through its fifty-eight pages and realized it was a journal. The first page declares it is "Ye Log of Ye Square Partie at Ye Great Brewster in ye pleasant month of July 1891." It was followed by a sketch of four dancing women in long skirts who proclaimed themselves to be the "Merrie Trippers" who "consisteth" of "Ye Autocrat, Ye Aristocrat, Ye Acrobat and Ye Scribe." He soon was mesmerized by the journal's entries, the photographs and the illustrations.

The authors of the Great Brewster journal recorded their entire seventeen-day sojourn on Great Brewster, including the meals they prepared, the household tasks they performed, the board games they played and the books they read. Their black-and-white photographs captured the wild beauty of their "enchanted Isle," yet the women also described getting regular deliveries of mail and milk and even entertaining guests who arrived by boat. The journal was both mysterious and precise; Stilgoe could see that the women were on a vacation from the men and families in their lives. And yet the document lacked one essential element. Nowhere were the women identified by name. It was if they had become their own literary creations, living a life that could last only for a fleeting moment.

Stilgoe's research focuses on the relationship between humans and their physical surroundings; he is the author of *What Is Landscape?* (2015) and *Old Fields: Photography, Glamour, and Fantasy Landscape* (2014), among other books. He realized the journal had immense historical value and was immediately worried that it would be purchased, taken apart and its pages sold individually on a place like eBay, a common practice for old ephemera. He was determined to prevent that. Stilgoe immediately arranged to have Harvard University buy the journal—putting up his own credit card as a guarantee. Eventually, in 1999, the journal became part of the collection of the Schlesinger Library of the Radcliffe Institute for Advanced Study, where it has become a prized artifact.

Stilgoe realized the women were special, by their economic status, education or other factors, which allowed them to take a vacation like this. What was more astonishing to him was how they were also able to capture

This excellent photo of the Great Brewster cottage from the journal is captioned "Ye Business End of Ye Home." It shows odd white patches on the ground, possibly laundry spread out to bleach and dry in the sun.

some of what they were seeing and feeling. "I'm not surprised the women were there—I'm surprised that they produced such a beautiful document," Stilgoe said in a 2009 interview for the *Harvard Gazette*.

Yet what this journal does *not* contain is also striking. There are no references to family, husbands or children, current events, politics or, indeed, life outside the island, aside from citations from books and poetry. Rather, the entries are colorful, emotive recordings of what the women were experiencing—this is less a private journal than a Facebook page of the 1890s. And, like Facebook, the document does not put the entries into context. The women mention places, games and books unfamiliar today. They cite names without really identifying the person, such as "William the Swede," "Mr. Dean" and "Ye Jolly Postman" and reference things like the "XV" without explaining this was a women's club with fifteen members. Most importantly, they never actually identify who they are or where they are from.

Still, this journal is a stunning capture of the lives of women at a pivotal time in the roles of American women. Granted, these women were from comfortable white families in the city of Lowell, Massachusetts, and were the daughters or wives of business owners, skilled craftsmen and mechanics. But wealth does not preclude obscurity. The records of even the richest and most culturally and politically active women of the 1890s and early twentieth century are miniscule compared to that of men of the era. Generally, the work and achievements of women were not considered on par with the accomplishments of men.

The journal came to the attention of Stephanie Schorow while she was doing research for her book *East of Boston: Notes from the Harbor Islands*, published by The History Press. She was enthralled and mystified by the document, which she examined in two visits to the Schlesinger Library. Schorow began to discuss the journal in her various lectures about the Boston Harbor Islands. Likewise, Suzanne Gall Marsh, the founder of the Friends of the Boston Harbor Islands and one of the area's foremost authorities on the history of the islands, became intrigued with the document. Both were determined to see that the journal was thoroughly researched and its treasures shared with a wider audience.

To that end, they organized a volunteer project for the Friends of the Boston Harbor Islands, a nonprofit that has advocated for the Harbor Islands since 1979. This group of volunteers began to transcribe, research and write the annotations and notes that contextualize the entries. Under the direction of Schorow, who has published eight books on Boston history, this cadre of women and one man worked to solve the journal's mysteries, not least of which was to determine the names and background of the women authors. Meeting by Zoom, the volunteers divided up tasks and began to dig.

The team included Ann Marie Allen, Allison Andrews, Vivian Borek, Elizabeth Carella, Carol Fithian, Walter Hope, Pam Indeck, Marguerite Krupp and Suzanne Gall Marsh. Carella, a trained curator of historic photography and expert on Rainsford Island, was able to help refine and interpret the photos. Special credit goes to Martha Mayo of Lowell, former director, University of Massachusetts Lowell, Center for Lowell History; she graciously shared her research. With her invaluable help, the team identified the four women with reasonable certainty and do for the journal what it cannot do on its own, that is, put its contents into context.

This book is the result of that work. With great thanks to the Schlesinger Library of Radcliffe, which gave permission for the project, and the cooperation of The History Press, this book reproduces most of the pages of the Great Brewster journal and puts the entries in context. Five preliminary chapters are followed by the entire transcript of the journal and as many

Taken from the side of the north drumlin, this photo from the journal shows two women looking over the island. A boat, perhaps belonging to William the Swede, is anchored offshore, and we can see the emergence of a spit of land that reaches into the harbor.

reproduced pages, photos and illustrations as could be included. The intention is to provide information on the women and their times, as well as the Boston Harbor Islands overall. A final chapter traces the history of Great Brewster Island in the twentieth and twenty-first centuries and how it is now part of the Boston Harbor Islands National and State Park, an unusual park that comprises thirty-four islands and peninsulas in the harbor.

This book is intended to be both a joyful summer read and a resource for women's studies departments, history departments and those engaged in scholarship on the history and culture of the Boston Harbor Islands. It is hoped that it will encourage readers, both young and old, to take on the art of "journaling," in which so-called ordinary people capture the events and texture of their lives and find that, indeed, their lives are extraordinary.

It's been an adventure to decipher the mysteries of the Great Brewster journal. The first challenge was to identify the four women who traveled to Great Brewster and discover why they went there. Here's how that was accomplished.

THE MERRIE TRIPPERS

Introducing the Women

With great élan, the four women in the journal dubbed themselves a "Square Partie," perhaps a reference to their number, as well as "The Merrie Trippers." They adopted a romanticized kind of argot for their journal. The first page of their journal declares it is "Ye Log of Ye Square Partie at Ye Great Brewster in Ye pleasant month of July 1891," and almost every caption after that is "Ye this" or "Ye that." (Add a few "aaarghs" and you'd think they were pirates.)

They use their monikers—Ye Autocrat of Great Brewster, Ye Gentle Aristocrat, Ye Artistic Acrobat and Ye Veracious Scribe—throughout the entries, and in only a few cases does a writer slip into using a first-person singular pronoun of "I" or "me." Their journal has elements of a diary, scrapbook and ship's log. The layout and structure indicate it may have been a document assembled after the trip from reconstructed notes and with developed and printed photographs added. This journal was likely a narrative meant to be shared among friends as a kind of a quasi-public document, even though the writers did not include their real names. One might imagine how surprised these women might be to learn that more than one hundred years later, a team of researchers pored over their handwriting and syntax.

What was first striking is how meticulously the women recorded their adventure. They added beautifully rendered floor plans of the cottage where they stayed, and the photographer(s) seemed to have carefully taken pictures of many of the rooms to create a thorough visual record. In particular,

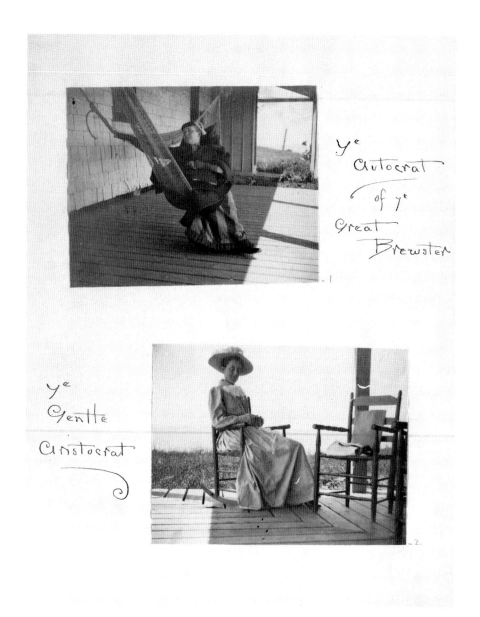

On this page and the next are the best photographs of the women in the journal and the only ones in which we get a sense of their faces. "Ye Autocrat of Ye Great Brewster" has been identified as Helen Frances Ray French and "Ye Gentle Aristocrat" as Sarah Elizabeth "Lizzie" Dean Adams.

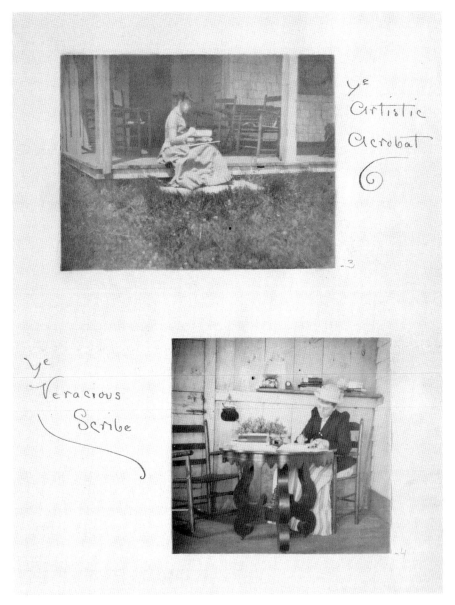

"Ye Artistic Acrobat" is likely Isabella "Bella" Coburn, a promising artist seen here at her craft. "Ye Veracious Scribe" is Helen Augusta Whittier, with hat and spectacles, writing something—perhaps even notes for this journal.

they took great pride in recording all their meals, from the main course to dessert and beverages. Certainly, some of the entries are fairly banal; they go on at length about their reactions to rain and sunshine. While they took lots of photos, there are no close-ups of the women individually, so their appearance remains a trifle elusive. They quote extensively from popular poetry of the day—John Greenleaf Whittier, Lord Byron and Alfred Lord Tennyson (and in one case some doggerel of their own)—but otherwise, the rest of the world doesn't intrude.

The identity of the writers might have remained forever a mystery but for a note that was attached to the document in the bookstore (and we still don't know how the journal wound up there). The note was on the stationery of Charles B. Nichols (1897–1984) of Hopkinton, New Hampshire. It described the journal as, "Interesting account of visit to Great Brewster Island in Boston Harbor. The ladies were friends of my mothers—the scribe Miss Helen Whittier." What Nichols was indicating was that the ladies were friends of his mother, Harriet Spalding Nichols (1865–1955), and he identified "the Scribe" as Helen Augusta Whittier (1846–1925). A signature on the last page of the journal is that of "Mrs. A.L. Tyler," whom we identified as Mrs. Artemas L. Tyler (Florence H. Whittier Tyler, 1862–1936), who was Helen A. Whittier's niece and only surviving relative. Helen Whittier's funeral services were held at Mrs. Tyler's house on Fairmount Street in Lowell. Perhaps Tyler owned the journal and gave it to Harriet Nichols, who passed it to her son.

Whittier has long been identified as the "Scribe" of the book. However, four women went on the adventure, hence a "Square Partie." There are four different handwriting styles in the journal. The photographs have captions but no credits. Some, but not all, of the small watercolors are signed with the initials of B.C. or H.A.W. These clues helped identify the women. Due to Whittier's prominent role in women's clubs of the day and her membership in two Lowell women's clubs, the Dickens Club and the XV Club, it seemed logical that the three other women were also members of those clubs. The first page of the journal is marked with a Roman numeral XV, rendered as a kind of logo, so this trip was likely some sort of club activity.

A great deal of information on Whittier and the two clubs was gleaned from an article published in the *Boston Globe* on March 13, 1893, titled "Lowell's Oldest Literary Club." The piece focused on the history of the XV Club, which may have been one of a number of XV clubs that sprang up around the country at this time. (A similar version of this article was also

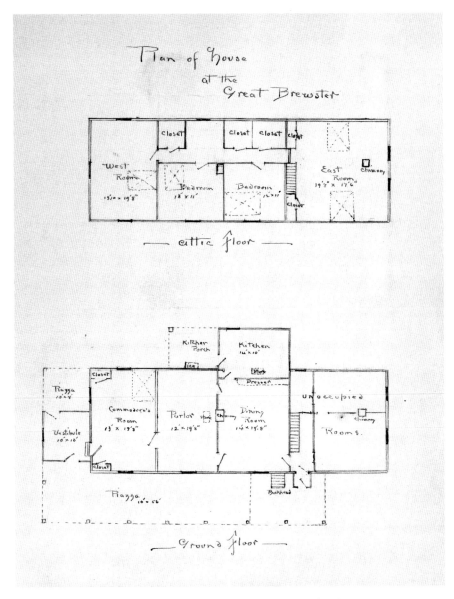

One of the unusual aspects of the journal is the systematic way that the women documented their sojourn, while at the same time frustrating today's readers by leaving out details, not least of which was their actual names. This careful rendering of the cottage floor plan shows a dining room and a parlor and something called the Commodore's Room. Note the lack of any kind of bathroom.

published in the *Globe* on March 25, 1906.) According to the article, Helen A. Whittier was a founding member of the Dickens Club in Lowell in 1869; initially, the club focused on reading and discussing works by Charles Dickens. Dickens visited Lowell in 1842 during the first of his two tours of the United States; he returned to the United States in 1867. Eventually, the club's interests expanded to include other literary works. According to the *Globe*, the Dickens Club evolved into the XV Club because it had fifteen members. The XV Club studied Chaucer, art history and the history and culture of Spain and Egypt. (Egyptology was a popular subject among late Victorians following the archaeological discoveries in the Valley of the Kings.) Members gave lectures, and each meeting began with a quotation from a selected poet. The club also took trips together to the homes of friends in the mountains and to the seashore. (See chapter 3 for more on women's clubs.)

The *Boston Globe* articles indicate the most memorable of the XV Club's outings "was a sojourn of two week's time on Great Brewster island in Boston Harbor, when nine members of the club successfully undertook cooperative housekeeping though so many 'miles from a lemon.'" The use of the term *cooperative housekeeping* is intriguing. The implication is that women came together to keep house without families or, more importantly, servants. The phrase *miles from a lemon* may have been a reference to the book *Twelve Miles from a Lemon* by Gail Hamilton, which itself was a reference to English writer Sydney Smith, who declared that his life in Yorkshire was so out of the way it was actually "twelve miles from a lemon." The article is hinting that the women were perfectly capable of running a home by themselves, even in a remote and isolated location. In fact, it's possible the article was written by one of the club members, possibly Helen Whittier herself. The article also references a trip of nine women, not the four of the Square Partie; the team suspected (and later confirmed) that there were at least two visits to Great Brewster by members of the XV Club, in 1879 and in 1891.

Through the names of the club members mentioned in the *Globe* article and skillful genealogy work by Martha Mayo of Lowell, the identities of the other three Merrie Trippers have been pinpointed with reasonable accuracy. The public records on Ancestry.com, especially census records, vital statistics and city directories, also provided information on the Trippers and people related to them and their adventure.

This photo from the journal is labeled "Morning on Ye Piazza" and shows three of the women on an outside porch. The photographer opted to position the women carefully and capture them in the middle of their tasks, such as sewing or perhaps sketching.

Helen Frances Ray French

Evidence indicates that the Autocrat was Helen Frances Ray French (1843–1921), a member of a notable Lowell family and a member of the XV Club. The journal notes that the women celebrated the birthday of the Autocrat on July 21. Massachusetts birth records show Helen Frances Ray was born in Lowell on July 21, 1843, to James Ray (1820–1854), a cap manufacturer, and Rachael McKee. Helen was one of seven siblings; she graduated from Lowell High School in 1857. Her father died at age thirty-four; her mother married John H. Wilkinson, and the family moved from Lowell to Roxbury, a community that later became part of Boston.

In 1869, at age twenty-six, Helen married Josiah Bowers French Jr. (1830–1901), the son of bank president and Lowell mayor Josiah Bowers French Sr. In the late 1850s, Josiah Bowers French Jr. moved to Chicago and opened a drugstore. After Helen and Josiah married in Lowell, they settled in Chicago for nearly ten years and then returned to Lowell before 1880. In 1880, Helen Frances Ray and her husband, Josiah Bowers French Jr., were living at 28 Chelmsford Street, former home of Lowell mayor Josiah Bowers French Sr. By 1890, they were landlords at the William Livingston stone mansion, 50 Chelmsford Street, which had been converted into a large lodging house. Helen French also lived in New York and Cambridge, Massachusetts. Helen French died on April 29, 1921, and was buried in the large French family lot in the Lowell Cemetery.

SARAH ELIZABETH DEAN ADAMS

Sarah Elizabeth "Lizzie" Dean Adams (1847–1918) was likely the Aristocrat. Her father was James Dean (1818–1875). Her mother was Sarah Bowers Chase (1818–1888). As a child in 1829, James Dean immigrated to the United States from Clitheroe, England, with his parents and family, including his younger brother Benjamin Dean. James and his father worked as block cutters and engravers for textile companies in Lowell; Providence, Rhode Island; and eventually Manchester, New Hampshire. Lizzie was the oldest daughter of eleven children, five boys and six girls. She graduated from Lowell High School in 1864. In 1869, she was a founding member of the Dickens Club and also a founding member of the XV Club in Lowell. Her uncle Benjamin Dean (1824–1897), a man active in local, state and national politics, likely influenced the Trippers' choice of Great Brewster for their retreat.

Benjamin Dean, who had family ties to at least two of the Merrie Trippers, purchased Outer Brewster Island from the City of Boston in 1871 and initiated a lease for Great Brewster Island in 1875. *Library of Congress; taken between 1870 and 1880.*

Benjamin Dean was an important figure in Massachusetts politics and in the life of the Boston Harbor Islands; he is frequently mentioned as "Mr. Dean" in the journal. Raised

The sloop *Clitheroe* owned by Benjamin Dean, who also owned the cottage that sheltered members of the XV Club in 1891 and 1879. *Courtesy of Historic New England.* Clitheroe, *June 27, 1890, "Goelet Cup for Sloops, 1890." Photograph by Nathaniel L. Stebbins.*

in Lowell, he later moved to Boston, where he was a prominent attorney and later a U.S. representative in Congress. He owned Outer Brewster Island and was one of the founders of the Boston Yacht Club in 1866 along with his brother Thomas Dean, Augustus and Charles Russ and Eben Denton. Additionally, Dean was chairman of the Boston Parks Commission (1885– 90) and president of the South Boston Gaslight Company. A resident of South Boston, he had a yacht called *Clitheroe*, which was named for his family's hometown in Lancashire, England.

Dean leased Great Brewster from the City of Boston for many years (according to *King's Handbook of Boston Harbor* and other sources), and there are mentions of a house he had there. A circa 1850 map from the U.S. Engineering Department shows a number of buildings, including a smithy, a stable and a one-and-a-half-story "boarding house," forty feet by twenty feet. A notation on the map says all the structures "were built in 1849." The boardinghouse may well be the house where the "Square Partie" enjoyed their adventure. Dean served as commodore of the Boston Yacht

Club, and there is a mention of the "Commodore's Room" in the Great Brewster house in the July 24 entry.

In 1875, Lizzie Dean married Landon S. Adams (1845–1925), paymaster for over thirty years at the Lowell Manufacturing Company, which produced beautiful broadloom carpets purchased by many elegant hotels throughout the United States and Europe. They lived on Market Street in Lowell for thirty years. They raised three children: Mary Dean Adams (1876–1955), Cecil Landon Adams (1878–1917) and Leslie Loren Adams (1882–1936). At age forty-four, with three young children at home (ages fifteen, thirteen and nine), Lizzie embarked on the Great Brewster trip.

ISABELLA COBURN

The Acrobat was likely the talented artist Isabella "Bella" Coburn (1849–1895). The initials and date "B.C. 91" appear on numerous watercolors and sketches in the journal. Her parents were Franklin Coburn (1817–1902), who worked as a clerk in his brother's West Indies goods store, and Hannah Estes Phelps (1822–1907). She was the second daughter of four siblings, one boy and three girls. As did the other Merrie Trippers, Bella attended Lowell High School, graduating in 1866. In 1867, she attended Lasell Female Seminary in Newton, Massachusetts, which was founded in 1851 as the Auburndale Female Seminary and became one of the first two-year colleges for women. (Lasell later became Lasell College and began admitting men in 1997. It is now Lasell University.) Her education continued and led to employment. She is listed as enrolled at the New England Conservatory of Music in 1868 and a decade later at the Massachusetts Normal Art School (now the Massachusetts College of Art and Design) where the Boston marine artist Walter Lofthouse Dean had studied a few years earlier. (Walter Dean was the son of Benjamin Dean Jr., which also made him the cousin of Bella's fellow Tripper Sarah Elizabeth "Lizzie" Dean Adams.) By the 1880s, city documents show Bella employed as a drawing instructor in Lowell's public schools. Along with her friend Helen Whittier, she was also hired to judge school art contests.

Bella Coburn and Helen Whittier were also exhibitors at the 1876 Centennial International Exhibition in Philadelphia. Their submissions were painted porcelain shown in the Women's Pavilion. This was an important event. It was America's first world's fair, designed to celebrate

Labeled "Ye Fort and Ye Narrows," this photo from the journal shows a sitting woman identified as the "Aristocrat" watching as a boat under full sail traverses the narrow channel at the end of the sandspit formed from Great Brewster Island at low tide.

the one hundredth anniversary of America's independence and showcase the country's many achievements in manufacturing, agriculture and the arts. Exhibits were housed in hundreds of buildings on acres of landscaped space, and thirty-seven countries participated. On display were the practical and luxurious commodities becoming more available in the nineteenth century. The fair was enormously popular, and nearly ten million people visited over the six-month duration.

Coburn never married. She taught in the Lowell Public Schools Free Hand, Machine and Architectural Drawing Program until 1890. On November 27, 1895, she died of heart failure at her family home, 757 Merrimack Street, Lowell, at age forty-six, about four years after the Great Brewster trip.

The women's connections ran far deeper than the Great Brewster trip. Some of them lodged at various times at 50 Chelmsford Street in Lowell, sometimes with other family members. Far from a typical factory boardinghouse, this grand home on Chelmsford Street belonged to the prosperous and politically prominent William Livingston family, and this living arrangement may have come through family connections to the Livingstons. Helen Frances Ray's husband, Josiah French Jr., grew up nearby at 28 Chelmsford Street. Sidney Spalding, father of Harriet Spalding Nichols, a dear friend of the Trippers, collaborated with Livingston in Lowell's earliest real estate development, according to *A History of Lowell* by Charles Cowley. Whether the families boarded together by choice or circumstance, it is an indication that they remained close, in proximity at least, after their island adventure.

While records on Bella Coburn, Lizzie Dean Adams and Helen Ray French are sparse, Helen A. Whittier is another matter.

THE REMARKABLE LIFE OF HELEN AUGUSTA WHITTIER, THE SCRIBE

Helen Whittier belonged to that group of young women whose girlhood was set in the dramatic years of the Civil War and from that hour woman's position in society was so altered that never again has the readjustment been so immediate, so far-reaching. Women under the stress of those tragic years struck off the fetters that had bound them. They saw opportunities for self expression through education, through social service and through a broader culture which might be brought about by the formation and foundation of clubs and organizations.
—Helen Augusta Whittier, 1846–1925: A Memorial,
by Mabel Hill, published 1930

An artist, a businesswoman, a teacher, a photographer, a civic leader and a proponent of women's suffrage, Helen Augusta Whittier—the Scribe—demonstrated a range of skills that would be breathtaking today and was truly astonishing in the nineteenth century. Whittier seemed to live with a fierce determination. She had business acumen—she was the sole woman to run a mill business in Lowell in her time. She was artistic—she was known for her skills painting porcelain and taking photographs. She was an organizer; beginning at age twenty-three, she helped organize and run women's clubs in Lowell and Boston and other locations throughout Massachusetts, using these institutions to further women's education and political status. There are numerous mentions of her lectures and talks in the newspapers of the day. One of the reasons for this book is to bring her life story to a wider audience and share her accomplishments in a way that was not possible during her lifetime.

Yet Helen's character remains elusive. She never married and seemed to have a lifelong friendship with fellow Lowell native Ella Taylor Wright (1849–1930), with whom she traveled the world in her later years. Although she likely kept a diary, as did many women of the day (she was, after all, nicknamed "The Scribe"), it has not surfaced. Her contemporary biographers tend to emphasize her gentle spirit and took pains to paint her as a warm, feminine presence. Typical is this description written by Mabel Hill in a memorial booklet written after Whittier's death in 1925 and published by the Massachusetts State Federation of Women's Clubs:

> *As one thinks of Miss Whittier in connection with publicity work through State and Federal enactments, one might gain the impression of a masculine mind and possibly a masculine personality, but one friend writes, "The abiding thought of Helen Whittier is of a gentle presence." And yet another friend writes that as she came into the meeting of the Federation, "One always felt a certain sense of reliance that in any subject under discussion she could be counted upon for good, sound service and quiet leadership."*

That booklet, the only full account of Whittier's life, is maddening; it substitutes florid descriptions for facts and seems to deliberately skirt specifics of Whittier's life and accomplishments. Still, it is the most complete account that we have found.

A photo of Helen as a young woman was published in the *Boston Globe* in a 1906 article on Lowell's XV Club (even though she was about sixty years old at the time). It shows an elegant young woman with strong features who seems both fresh and sure of herself. A later, more formal portrait of her used in various other publications seems stiff and uncharacteristically rigid. A photo of her in later life shows a woman proudly sporting glasses with lace at her neck and hair piled on her head. The effect is somewhat severe, but there's a smile about to break out on her lips, and her eyes are clear and penetrating. The Scribe, as portrayed in the Great Brewster journal, seemed a woman of great possession. That may have been driven, in part, by her upbringing.

Helen was born in 1846 in Lowell, the only daughter of Moses Whittier and Lucindia Blood to survive into adulthood. Three years after giving birth to her first child, Henry, Lucindia gave birth to a daughter who died the same day that she was born. Helen's other sister, Elizabeth, died at the age of six, several months before Helen's birth.

Right: Helen Augusta Whittier was the daughter of Moses Whittier, who founded the Whittier Cotton Mill Company in Lowell. She later took over the operation of the mill. *Stephanie Schorow collection.*

Below: Kirk Street facing French Street in Lowell, where Helen A. Whittier grew up. Her family's house was on the left. *Courtesy of University of Massachusetts Lowell Libraries, Center for Lowell History, Photograph Collection [John Goodwin].*

Helen's father was an enterprising man. Moses Whittier was born on April 16, 1795, in Canaan, New Hampshire. After spending his childhood on the family farm, Moses moved to Maine, where he was employed as a machinist, a jeweler and, eventually, a mechanic and cotton mill supervisor. In the early 1830s, Moses moved to Lowell, Massachusetts, to work as a supervisor and overseer at the Merrimack Manufacturing Company, the first textile company in the United States to produce printed calico cloth. Shortly after arriving in Lowell, he married Lucindia Blood in 1832. In 1836, while living in Lowell with his young family, Moses left the Merrimack Manufacturing Company and became a supervisor/overseer at the newly opened Boott Cotton Mills. In 1852, he established the Whittier Cotton Mill Company, which manufactured loom harness equipment for other textile companies. About 1865, Moses resigned from the Boott Cotton Mills to focus on his own company, and in 1867, he and his son, Henry, reorganized and established the Whittier and Son Company, which produced heavy twine. Moses retired in 1875, leaving his son as sole owner.

Helen Augusta Whittier grew up in Lowell with her brother, Henry, who was fourteen years her senior. Their life seemed comfortable but not extravagant. Even as a child, Helen demonstrated the skills and talents that would sustain her through her life. From an early age, she appears to have prized education, art and literature. Helen entered Lowell High School at age twelve. In 1862, she won the Carney Medal for scholarship and character, an honor given to only a few students each year. Employing the social blinders of the day, Mabel Hill calls Whittier a product of "good blood, good breeding, with notable pioneers and civic leaders of New England life" and notes that she was "brought up to believe in plain living, together with big and broad thinking. There was also a vision of service and responsibility."

After finishing high school, Helen Whittier attended Lasell Female Seminary (now the coed Lasell University) as a student of art and art history. After graduation, she taught china painting at the Lowell Evening Drawing Program and organized a Tile Club for painting fireplace tiles that were fired in the group's own kiln. In 1876, Whittier was selected to participate in the national Philadelphia Centennial Exposition for her china painting—a prestigious honor. Also participating in the exhibit was Bella Coburn, the "Artistic Acrobat" of the Merrie Trippers, another indication of the deep ties among the women on the Great Brewster trip.

In 1878, Whittier was a founding board member of the Lowell Art Association (now housed at the Whistler House Museum of Art in Lowell), considered one of the oldest art associations in the country.

WHITTIER AS A BUSINESSWOMAN

Whittier ventured out of areas traditionally reserved for women and became a pioneer in another area—the world of manufacturing and business. In 1879, four years after their father's retirement, Helen's brother, Henry, opened the newly constructed Whittier Mill on Stackpole Street in Lowell near the confluence of the Concord and Merrimack Rivers. The mill manufactured twine, fire hose cord and weaving and knitting yarns. After Henry's death of kidney disease in 1888 at the age of fifty-five, Helen assumed control of the company with the assistance of her cousin Nelson Whittier, who supervised operations at the mill. Throughout the textile industry, Helen Whittier was acknowledged and acclaimed as the only woman head of a major textile company in the United States. To see a postcard of the Whittier Mill in Lowell, see the color midsection of this book.

While Whittier came from a comfortable background, there is some evidence that she suffered a financial setback after taking over the mill. In 1893—just two years after the Great Brewster trip—the United States spiraled into an economic crisis. During the so-called Panic of 1893, the stock market tumbled, banks and businesses went bankrupt, unemployment shot up and credit essentially froze. It was the country's largest economic crisis thus far and would be surpassed only by the Great Depression.

According to Mabel Hill, Whittier Mills faced financial ruin; creditors told Helen that "even her home had to be sacrificed to meet the losses." Paul Butler and Charles B. Stevens became the primary stockholders of Whittier Mills, which continued to operate until 1901. It's unclear exactly how badly Helen Whittier was financially affected. Mabel Hill, in another of her maddening flights of fancy, dwelt on Whittier's can-do spirit:

> At the moment that she might have brooded upon her losses and faced the future with dread, she caught sight of a glorious sunset across the fields, the most beautiful sunset she had ever seen, so she often said afterwards to her intimate friend who has recorded this story....She was ready to go on, ready to readjust herself into a woman who should earn her living by teaching those things that heretofore had belonged to her world of leisure.

As did other mills of the time, Whittier Mills expanded its operations by opening a mill in Georgia in January 1896. The city of Atlanta had hosted several cotton expositions for the purpose of attracting business investments. Companies from the North were attracted to the South for its proximity to raw materials, thus lowering transportation costs, its lower wages, fewer restrictions on labor, and tax breaks. Whittier Cotton Company selected a site about six miles outside the city of Atlanta along the banks of the Chattahoochee River and near the Southern Railway. The company negotiated a deal with the Chattahoochee Brick Company to buy thirty acres of land and for Chattahoochee to provide bricks for the mill and build housing for workers.

Although the Whittier family did not own the mill at this point, they served as its officers. Helen Whittier was president, her cousin Nelson Whittier was treasurer and his son Walter Rufus Boyden Whittier, the "Boss," was manager. Later, Walter's sons, Paul and Sidney, would run the mill. Helen was the public face of the mill. Its opening was reported in newspapers throughout the state of Georgia. Typical of the accounts is that reported in the *Athens Banner* on Friday morning, January 10, 1896:

> *ATLANTA, Jan 7—The Whittier cotton mills, located on the Chattahoochee river, six miles from this city, were set in operation. Miss Helen A. Whittier, daughter of the president of the company, pressed an electric button and put the spindles in operation, opening up another great industry for Atlanta and giving employment to between 300 and 400 people.*
>
> *The construction of the mills was begun last spring and finished a week ago. The total cost was $200,000. The mill has 10,000 spindles and is one of the finest equipped factories in the country.*

It is interesting to note that, despite her father having died twelve years earlier and her brother eight years earlier, the article does not properly identify Helen as president of the mill in her own right.

The Atlanta mill operated seven days a week with two twelve-hour shifts: midnight to noon and noon to midnight. By 1900, according to the U.S. Census, there were 635 employees at the mill, many of them children. Massachusetts had passed a compulsory school attendance law in 1852—the first in the nation—Georgia did not pass such a law until 1916, which left many children available as a source of inexpensive labor. According to Michael Schuman, author of "History of Child Labor in the United States—Part 1: Little Children Working," published by the U.S. Bureau of Labor Statistics in the January 2017 *Monthly Labor Review*, child labor was widely used in a number of industries, with cotton milling "most prominent among the child-labor-intensive industries."

A portrait of Helen Augusta Whittier in her later years. *Courtesy of the Schlesinger Library.*

As far as can be determined, the Whittier Mills in Lowell did not use child labor at this time; however, the lifestyles and quality of life of the mill workers clearly differed from that of the Whittier family and their social circle.

In the 1930s, the Georgia mill struggled through the Great Depression and the General Textile Strike of 1934, after which Walter R.B. "Boss" Whittier left the company. Sidney Whittier, the last Whittier to be president of the mill, was replaced in 1936. The mill's fortunes revived somewhat during the Second World War but again floundered through several ownership changes before it finally closed in 1971, the casualty of domestic and international competition. The empty buildings were damaged by arson in 1986. The mill's water tower still stands on the site as part of a seventeen-acre city park with a plaque commemorating the mill and its residential village. The workers' houses have been renovated and are now private homes within a designated historic district. The structure that housed the Whittier Mills on Stackpole Street in Lowell now serves as public housing managed by Lowell Housing Authority.

Even if the *Athens Banner* did not note Whittier's accomplishments as a businesswoman, other media did. In 1899, an article on Helen Whittier written by a women's club colleague of hers, Helen M. Winslow, in the *Delineator*, a popular sewing and patterns magazine, said:

> *Miss Whittier is in some ways a remarkable woman. Her father was the president for many years of the Whittier Cotton Mills of Lowell, the largest part of which was owned by himself. When age crept on and his duties became onerous his daughter Helen, educated to the highest degree, reared in luxury and popular with everyone so that had she chosen, she might have been the gayest of society butterflies, went into her father's office as his helper. For several years she was his "right hand" so that when the head of the Whittier Mills was finally taken to his long home, she was unanimously chosen to fill his place as being the only person in the world who fully understood the management of the mills.*

Frances Willard, known for her ardent support of women's suffrage and her unwavering push for temperance, published an 1897 book on *Occupations for Women*, which specifically cited Whittier:

> *She is said to be the only woman president of a big cotton factory in this country. She is a finely educated and highly refined woman, mistress of all the so-called "accomplishments" and president of one of the largest women's clubs in the country. Miss Whittier, with her gentle, quiet ways*

and wonderful business ability, is a fine example of what the true American businesswoman may become.

Again, the contemporary eye is struck with how Whittier, despite her powerful positions, is frequently described as a highly refined, gentle and quiet woman.

Census data indicate that in 1893, Whittier moved from the family home on Kirk Street in Lowell to 50 Chelmsford Street, a large boardinghouse, described in chapter 1. (Three of the Merrie Trippers also lived in this location at various times.) She began teaching art history at Bradford Female Academy, Bradford, Massachusetts, and lectured at women's clubs on art, architecture and sculpture. We found many references to these lectures in the *Boston Globe* archives.

WHITTIER AS A CIVIC LEADER

Whittier remained among the more influential leaders in the city of Lowell. In 1884, she, Martha Coburn and six men, incorporated the Channing Fraternity, a Unitarian organization designed to aid the poor and provide lectures, concerts and theatrical entertainment. In 1895, Whittier served on the Middlesex Mechanics Association Committee along with Alexander Cumnock in developing a proposal for the creation of the Lowell Textile School (now University of Massachusetts Lowell).

Whittier would play a role in women's clubs over several decades, despite her own changes in fortunes. In 1894 (a few years after the Brewster trip), the Middlesex Women's Club of Lowell was launched, and in two years, Whittier was elected president. This club provided study classes and university extension work, with lectures by acknowledged experts. In 1899, the *Delineator* reported that the Middlesex Women's Club had "numbers upward of seven hundred members with a long waiting list, and although there are other small clubs in the 'City of Spindles,' this is the one everybody wants to join." As Middlesex Women's Club president, Whittier declared in her annual address of 1897 that the club's aim would be to study the conditions of society, not just focus on attempts for improvement: "It is coming to be recognized as one of the responsibilities of a woman's life that she should be informed of the fundamental principles upon which the social structure is reared."

In 1903, another phase of Whittier's life began. She moved to Dartmouth Street in Boston, where she collaborated with May Alden Ward as founders and editors of the General Federation of Women's Clubs newsletter, the *Federation Club Bulletin*. According to Hill:

> *Miss Whittier now found herself in the midst of a group of contemporaries who were women of action as well as expressing Victorian thought[,] a long list of women whose names are famous in Massachusetts as devoted workers for suffrage, for the upholding of parliamentary law, for the spread of lectures on current events, a long list indeed, if we should enumerate them all. These new friends had not only a forceful influence upon Miss Whittier's life after she went to Boston, but each in turn gained from Miss Whittier refreshment as from an eager soul who came quietly into their midst with a vivid and vital desire to serve.*

Whittier soon became one of the more powerful women in the women's club movement. She was a friend to Julia Ward Howe, the ardent abolitionist who composed "The Battle Hymn of the Republic" and founded the Massachusetts State Federation of Women's Clubs in 1893. Whittier became president of the federation in 1904 and served until 1907. In her first report, she stressed "Unity in Diversity" with this statement: "We ask the clubs for one thing—a widely diffused interest in Federation work." At the time, according to a history of the federation, there was widespread discussion about the inclusion of clubs with Black members.

Whittier was also involved in the early women's rights movement. In 1916, she served as the state director of the Massachusetts Woman Suffrage Association (MWSA), an organization devoted to women's suffrage from 1870 to 1919. We should recall that giving women the right to vote was a keenly controversial issue. The daughter of fellow Tripper Elizabeth Dean Adams was a well-known opponent of women's suffrage. Mary Dean Adams, while a New York immigration inspector, wrote anti-suffrage pamphlets, and in February 1909, she read a paper at the suffrage hearings in the capital of Albany arguing against votes for women. Part of her opposition was that this would give immigrant women the right to vote as well; she asserted that immigrant woman "would be as capable of understanding just about as much of political matters as a man deaf and blind would of the opera," according to *The Right to Vote: Rights and Liberties Under the Law* by D. Grier Stephenson. The Nineteenth Amendment, nonetheless, was ratified on August 18, 1920.

WHITTIER'S PERSONAL LIFE

It is tempting to read between the lines on aspects of Whittier's life. Mabel Hill described Whittier's devotion to an unidentified lifelong female friend, who may have provided many biographical details. This friend is believed to be Ella Taylor Wright, who was born in Lowell and died in Cleveland, Ohio. Both women attended Lowell High School and were members of the XV Club. Even when Wright moved to Ohio, the friends remained close. Whittier gifted Wright two photo albums of their time together in New England, according to material researcher Martha Mayo, found at the Cleveland History Center, Western Reserve Historical Society.

Later in life, Wright and Whittier traveled together extensively and summered together in Westford, Massachusetts. Yet Hill never names Wright, instead writing such descriptions as: "Both Miss Whittier and her friend were spiritually minded. She herself was a broad-minded Unitarian who saw life from the Emersonian point of view and from a (William Ellery) Channing education; the friend, a devoted churchwoman, a follower of Bishop (Phillips) Brooks." (Channing and Brooks were noted liberal theologians of their day; Brooks oversaw the building of Trinity Church in Boston's Copley Square.) The women were clearly close, but the precise nature of their relationship cannot be determined. Certainly, Whittier never married; however, many unmarried women of this era formed households with other women. This so-called Boston marriage was a term for a living arrangement between two women for financial or, occasionally, romantic reasons. Another factor in both Whittier's single status and that of fellow Tripper Bella Coburn might have been a lack of eligible men due to the death toll of the Civil War. Note that Louisa May Alcott (1832–1888), roughly a contemporary of the Merrie Trippers, railed against the restraints of nineteenth-century women's lives and also never married.

What marked Whittier's later life was a love for travel often taken with Wright. She first traveled to Europe in 1897 and made another trip in 1914, when she visited France and Italy. She and Wright later traveled to the Far East and China. Passport records confirm these trips, which were taken when Whittier was nearing seventy years of age. Apparently, the spirit of adventure that motivated her Great Brewster trips lasted the rest of her life. Hill writes:

> *Miss Whittier loved nature and during the last seven years of her life she was close to the heart of nature with its wonderful beauty all about her.*

Her friend, the dear friend with whom she had first traveled through Europe and later had crossed the Pacific to wander through China, had had the good fortune to inherit in the latter years of her life a stately old home in Westford, Massachusetts. Here these two beloved women spent the summer months together. Here Miss Whittier's love for nature gave her not only an expanding delight in flowers, trees, and the green grass of fields and lawn, but God Himself seemed very near to her. The Imminent Creator talked to her through blossoms, the west wind, and singing bird.

Whittier died on October 11, 1925, a woman respected and loved by her fellow club members and who now enjoyed the right to vote. A few years later, the Massachusetts State Federation of Women's Clubs established a Helen A. Whittier Scholarship at the University of Massachusetts Amherst, which has continued to be awarded.

The themes that appear in the Great Brewster journal—the joy of friends and fellowship, the beauty of the natural world, the ability of women to fend for themselves—were themes woven throughout Whittier's life. The journal's snippets of daily activities, the photographs (many likely taken by Whittier, see chapter 4), the evocative watercolors, and the loving care in which the journal was assembled were all reflections of Whittier's engaged, active life.

3

FROM THE SPINDLE CITY
TO WOMEN'S CLUBS

THE CITY OF LOWELL: "ART IS THE HANDMAID OF HUMAN GOOD" (CITY MOTTO)

In addition to friendship, the women shared a deep bond through the city of Lowell. They were raised and lived in Lowell, and all attended Lowell High School. Located about thirty miles north of Boston, Lowell was incorporated in 1826 and named in memory of Francis Cabot Lowell, who had established the first small textile mill in Waltham, Massachusetts. The area had once been home to members of the Pawtucket and Pennacook tribes for thousands of years; their population was significantly reduced by an epidemic around 1619, after Europeans arrived (see Rebecca Beatrice Brooks, author and publisher of the *History of Massachusetts* blog https://historyofmassachusetts.org). In the 1820s, the area around the powerful Pawtucket Falls on the Merrimack River in East Chelmsford, Middlesex County, was selected by early investors as the location for the first textile manufacturing center in the United States. Lowell's ten large textile companies produced thousands of yards of wool and cotton cloth and carpets sold throughout the United States and exported overseas. Dozens of mid-size and smaller companies were also established, producing textile machinery, power turbines, railroad locomotives and manufacturing equipment.

John Greenleaf Whittier (1807–1892), an abolitionist, writer and poet born in Haverhill, Massachusetts, was living in Lowell in the 1840s when he wrote "The City of a Day":

> *This, then, is Lowell,—a city springing up, like the enchanted palaces of the Arabian tales, as it were in a single night, stretching far and wide its chaos of brick masonry and painted shingles, filling the angle of the confluence of the Concord and the Merrimac with the sights and sounds of trade and industry. Marvelously, here have art and labor wrought their modern miracles.*

John Greenleaf Whittier's work seemed to be popular among the Merrie Trippers, who quote twice from his poem "The Tent on the Beach" in their journal. Interestingly, John Greenleaf Whittier was good friends with Lucy Larcom, a Lowell mill girl for ten years who later became a poet and teacher. Her poetry is also among the works lovingly cited by the Merrie Trippers in their journal (See July 29). The four women surely knew about the mill girls of their city.

To find workers for their mills in early Lowell, the textile corporations recruited women from New England farms and villages, according to "The Mill Girls of Lowell," published by the Lowell National Park Service at www.nps.gov. These women, many from farming families throughout New England, lacked other economic opportunities, and many were enticed by the prospect of monthly cash wages and room and board. Beginning in 1823, many women moved to Lowell to work in the mills. Although they faced long hours and hard work, many of them saved money and gained a measure of economic independence.

Another famous writer—Charles Dickens—became enamored of Lowell. The novelist visited Boston in 1842, during the first of two iconic trips to the United States. He took a train from Boston to Lowell, which he found to be "a large, populous, thriving place." As he later wrote in his *American Notes for General Circulation*, Dickens found Lowell "new" and "fresh."

> *The very river that moves the machinery in the mills (for they are all worked by water power), seems to acquire a new character from the fresh buildings of bright red brick and painted wood among which it takes its course; and to be as light-headed, thoughtless, and brisk a young river, in its murmurings and tumblings, as one would desire to see.*

This photo from the July 18 entry in the journal is labeled "Ye Capacious Ice Chest," referring to the large white box at the right where food was kept cold with ice. More interesting is how the two women in this photo—either preparing a meal or cleaning up—resemble servants. The Lowell women on this adventure were relatively well-off and probably had servants to do daily tasks such as meal preparation. On this trip, however, the Merrie Trippers seem to take delight in doing everything for themselves.

Dickens was particularly interested in the city's industries and visited a "woolen factory, a carpet factory, and a cotton factory." He wrote in detail about the "mill girls," finding them "all well dressed: and that phrase necessarily includes extreme cleanliness."

THE EMERGENCE AND IMPACT OF WOMEN'S CLUBS

Charles Dickens's fascination with their city stimulated the interest of the women of Lowell after he again toured the United States in 1867. Two years later, the Dickens Club was organized by a group of eight young women, all recent graduates of Lowell High School, including Helen Whittier and Elizabeth Dean—two of the Trippers. According to an account published in the *Boston Globe* on March 13, 1893, and other sources, the original members also included Ella Wood (president), Lilla Lawson, Annie A. Burke, Martha E. Blanchard, Anna F. Anderson and Helen Kimball. The women studied the works of Charles Dickens but soon branched out to other literary works. It was a chance for them to experience the kind of scholarship and discussion open primarily to men. Educational improvement groups had a long tradition in Lowell. Several were established in the 1840s.

In the late nineteenth century, women had few avenues for formal advanced studies in either the arts or sciences. Wellesley College, one of the country's most prestigious all-women colleges, opened in 1870, while Radcliffe College opened in Cambridge in 1879. Most major colleges of the day did not admit women. For many women of this era, women's clubs were a way for them to engage in scholarship and civic discourse. Club members were also part of a general movement supporting more rights for women; however, not all women's clubs were devoted to the issue of suffrage. They often promoted the concept of women's "sense of duty" and how women were the "most willing and joyful of martyrs," according to *The History of the Woman's Club Movement in America* by Jennie June Croly, published in 1889. Yet supporters of women's clubs saw the organizations as having an outsized influence. Croly fervently describes her vision for these organizations thus:

> *The women's club was not an echo; it was not the mere banding together for a social and economic purpose, like the clubs of men. It became at once, without deliberate intention or concerted action, a light-giving and seed-sowing centre of purely altruistic and democratic activity....It brought together qualities rather than personage; and by a representation of all interests, moral, intellectual, and social, a natural and equal division of work and opportunity, created an ideal basis of organization, where everyone has an equal right to whatever comes to the common centre....This is no ideal or imaginary picture. It is the simplest prose of every woman's club and every clubwoman's experience during the past thirty years.*

Women's clubs flourished from 1896 to 1916. In 1890, the General Federation of Women's Clubs was founded, bringing together about three thousand clubs with over one million members from around the country. One of the oldest women's clubs on record is the New England Women's Club, launched in 1868 to provide women with a forum to learn and have a voice on social reform. The Massachusetts State Federation of Women's Clubs, launched in 1893, had as many as three hundred affiliated clubs.

So it was not unusual for the Lowell women to band together into a social organization. The Dickens Club was eventually renamed the XV Club and may have been a Lowell version of what appears to be a national XV Club movement. According to the online Encyclopedia of Arkansas, the first XV Club was organized in 1879 in Bowling Green, Kentucky, and a XV chapter was later set up in Little Rock, Arkansas. "The fifteen members of the XV Club meet fifteen times a year for dinner and discussion of various important and interesting issues," and the name is pronounced "ex-VEE." This Little Rock club was for men. Further research by team member Martha Mayo finds that Haverhill, Massachusetts, had a XV Club chapter for women. The *Official Register and Directory of Women's Clubs in America* of 1914, edited by Helen M. Winslow (who also wrote the *Delineator* article on Helen Whittier) lists an "X.V. Club" in Albia, Iowa. It is difficult to determine if there was any kind of formal connection between the XV of Lowell and the others; a March 13, 1893, article in the *Boston Globe* indicates the Lowell club was called the XV because the membership was limited to fifteen.

According to the *Globe*, members of the XV Club in Lowell as of 1893 were Helen Whittier, Isabella Coburn, Helen F. French, Elizabeth Dean Adams (the four Merrie Trippers), Martha C. Walker (president), Alice J. Chase, Anna F. Anderson, Elizabeth W. Anderson, May M. Bement, Martha E. Blanchard, Annie Blanchard, Florence Wheaton, Grace A. Wood and Ella T. Wright. "Honorary" members were Lilla Lawson Grant, Alice Coburn Stevens, Alice Appleton Knowles, Julia D. Nesmith, Annie A. Burke and Dora Tucker Woodman.

Whittier and her friends envisioned the XV Club in Lowell to be more than a social gathering opportunity. "Miss Whittier felt that the members of her 'XV' should study, really study, as if in college with their brothers who were supposed to be scholarly," Mabel Hill wrote in her account of Whittier's life. Whittier approached Anna Eliot Ticknor (1823–1896) of Boston, a pioneer in home study or correspondence schools. Ticknor founded the Society to Encourage Studies at Home, which aimed "to induce among ladies the habit of devoting some part of every day to study of a systematic and thorough kind." Ticknor was a member of Boston's intellectual elite and the daughter of George Ticknor (a critic, historian and one of the original organizers of the Boston Public Library). Hill wrote that Whittier visited Anna Ticknor and convinced her to help the XV Club with home-study courses. Thus, according to the 1893 *Globe* article, the women began an intensive period of scholarship. They studied:

The works of Motley, Parkman and Justin McCarthy. Considerable time was given to old English literature, from Chaucer down. Six years were spent on the history of art under the guidance of the Study at Home society of Boston, which loaned valuable books and photographs. Later a study of Egypt and Spain was begun. When a member read a paper on Columbus, another gave a short account of the ideas of cosmography prevalent in his day and a paper on Philip II was accompanied by a sketch of the Escurial. Each meeting was opened by quotations from some poet selected for the day.

This indicates that the poetry and citations found throughout the Great Brewster journal were not random; they likely reflected the XV Club's intensive course of education. Thus, the journal is a kind of syllabus of what educated women were reading—and what they may have memorized—during this period. Even if none of the women received what might be called formal higher education, they certainly were well versed in the literature of the day.

4

WHY GREAT BREWSTER ISLAND?

The Early History of the Island

O f all the lovely places in New England to visit, why did the women choose Great Brewster? The answer likely lies in the freedom an island promised and the chance to challenge oneself in an environment of wildness and beauty. Each of the Boston Harbor Islands, although within view of the city and familiar landscapes, retains its own unique natural structure and history. Each draws visitors with its own gifts and challenges. There were also direct family connections between two of the Trippers and the man who leased Great Brewster.

Most of the inner islands that dot Boston Harbor were created by receding glaciers which plowed mounds of dirt and debris into hills known technically as drumlins. When sea levels rose, the drumlins became "drowned," making the harbor the only place in the United States with a "drowned drumlin field." This is clearly evident on Great Brewster. Some of the other outer islands in the harbor are largely bedrock with a thin coating of soil.

Before the arrival of Europeans, Indigenous people used the islands for seasonal living, fishing, hunting, refuge from storms and other transient purposes. The early European settlers found the islands to be a source of timber for the building of Boston and a place for farming and creating defenses for the new town.

Many of the islands were named for prominent early settlers. A group of four of the outermost islands were named Great (or Greater), Little, Middle and Outer Brewster after Elder William Brewster. A seventy-five-foot-tall lighthouse known as Boston Light was built in 1716 on Little Brewster, making it the oldest lighthouse station in the country. The lighthouse itself was destroyed in 1776, when the British made a retreat from Boston during the Revolutionary War. The lighthouse was rebuilt in 1783 and remains in operation today.

Great Brewster Island, the largest of the Brewsters, seems to have maintained its largely bucolic role. (*King's Handbook* indicates it was twenty-five acres; today the National Park Service records Great Brewster as nineteen acres upland.) George Worthylake, the first keeper of Boston Light from 1716 to 1718, kept a flock of sheep on Great Brewster Island. At low tide, the sheep could travel across the sandbar/mussel bed connecting Lighthouse Island (Little Brewster Island) with Great Brewster. "Fifty-nine of his sheep were caught on another long sand spit off Great Brewster during a 1717 storm, and they drowned when the tide came in," according to *Boston Light: Three Centuries of History 1716–2016* by Jeremy D'Entremont. Great Brewster has two sandspits that emerge at low tide. One reaches to Little Brewster. The other extends 1½ miles toward Georges Island and had a beacon called Narrows Light to warn mariners about shallow water. Today's navigational charts call this "the Great Brewster Spit."

A 1776 "Chart of the Harbour of Boston" indicates there are trees on the island along with "the beacon at the end of the sand spit." This beacon was operated separately from Boston Light. In 1856, this Narrows Light, also known as Bug Light, was built on the same spot as the 1776 beacon to warn mariners of Hardings (or Harding's) Ledge and the one-and-a-half-mile-long Great Brewster sandspit.

In the years following the American Revolution, and even up to the 1950s, Bostonians generally used the Boston Harbor Islands, particularly those in the inner harbor, as dumping grounds for people and things they did not want near or in the city. As Pavla Šimková writes in *Urban Archipelago*, her environmental history of the Boston Harbor Islands:

> *In the latter part of the nineteenth century, Boston was quickly running out of places to put its nuisances, its offensive trades, and the undesirable public institutions. As the settlement grew denser and the population more outspoken, the siting of unwelcome businesses and institutions was becoming increasingly difficult. There was however, still one wedge of the city's space that seemed underutilized and perfectly suited for such a purpose: the harbor islands.*

This photo shows the Narrows or "Bug" Lighthouse. It was completed in 1856 on the edge of the Great Brewster sandspit to warn mariners of the rocks at Harding's Ledge. It is an unusual screw-pile design.

The islands were used as sites for prisons, almshouses, reformatories, quarantine stations, hospitals, a horse-rendering plant and, in the case of Spectacle Island, a general garbage dump. Some islands, such as Georges, Peddocks and Lovells, were sites of major forts, created at a time when sea power was deemed a necessary coastal defense. Deer Island was once used as a kind of concentration camp for Christian Indigenous people during King Philip's (or Metacom's) War (1675–76). A prison was built there in 1896. For a more complete history of the islands, see *Discovering the Boston Harbor Islands*, by Christopher Klein, or *East of Boston: Notes from the Harbor Islands* by Stephanie Schorow.

The outer islands, however, were spared the fate of many of the inner islands. Fishing communities existed during the 1800s on Outer and Middle Brewster, Calf, Green, Long and Bumpkin Islands. The fisherfolk lived in simple huts and cabins built from driftwood. Around 1840, fishermen and their families began to move to the outer islands, although they generally had no ownership. After the Civil War, the rise of an upper-middle-class population allowed people the luxury of leisure time. Those of more ample means began to consider the islands, the Hull peninsula and the Hingham shore as a vacation destination, with hotels being built and excellent ferry service provided to get there.

In 1848, the City of Boston purchased Great Brewster for $4,000 from Lemuel Brackett. The city ceded a portion of the island to the U.S. government to build a seawall. The project was overseen by Colonel Sylvanus Thayer, the chief engineer for the Army Corps of Engineers Boston area. He was also responsible for overseeing the construction of Fort Warren on Georges Island and Fort Independence on Castle Island. Stonemasons were working on this seawall during the Trippers' visit.

An 1853 *Map of Great Brewster Island, Boston Harbor Showing the Abrasion from 1820–1851 Inclusive* indicates a stone pier, an office and store house, a one-and-a-half-story boardinghouse, a stable, a smithy and the Old House of Refuge for Mariners. It is believed that this "Old House" was part of the Massachusetts Humane Society's hut of refuge system established in 1786. Huts of refuge, stocked with food and clothing, sheltered survivors of shipwrecks until they could be rescued. Huts of refuge were also built on Lovells and Calf Islands. This "abrasion" has continued, at a rate estimated to be about three feet per decade.

Exactly what was happening on and to Great Brewster in the 1890s remains a bit murky, despite information in 1880 *Illustrated History of Boston Harbor* by James Henry Stark, the 1882 *King's Handbook of Boston Harbor* and the writings of Edward Rowe Snow. Like many elements of the islands' history, the official record is hard to piece together. What is clear is that the Brewsters were a kind of playground for wealthy citizens of Boston.

In 1876, Benjamin Dean, a founding member of the Boston Yacht Club, negotiated an exclusive lease for Great Brewster Island for the club for one hundred dollars. "It was used as a rendezvous point for picnics and outings. Exclusive control of the island was soon given up because it was deemed a useless expenditure. Since relatively few people had yachts, Great Brewster was de facto an exclusive place for yachtsmen. Why pay rent?" according to *The Boston: A History of the Boston Yacht Club, 1866–1979* by Paul E. Shanabrook. James Henry Stark reported, "The cottage seen on the island is the summer residence of the Hon. Benjamin Dean, who leased the island from the city. On Middle Brewster is a handsome square cottage which is the summer residence of Mr. Augustus Russ."

According to the 1882 *King's Handbook of Boston Harbor*, "The Great Brewster, the innermost Island, is mainly composed of a lofty and conspicuous bluff, half of which has been eaten away by the sea. It covers about twenty-five

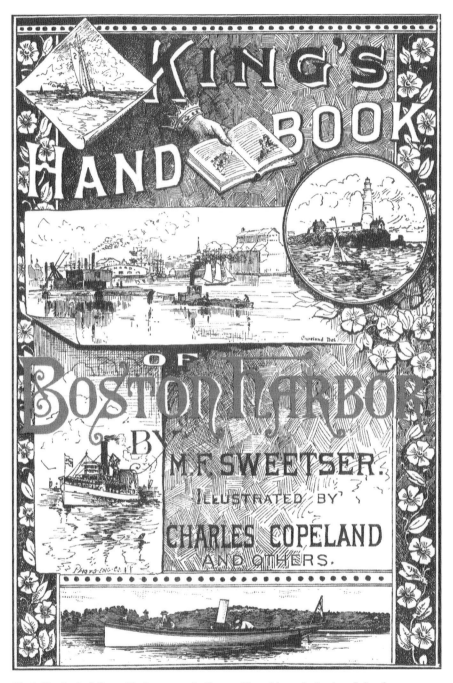

King's Handbook of Boston Harbor was an indispensable guide to the harbor. It has been republished by the Friends of the Boston Harbor Islands. *Courtesy of Friends of the Boston Harbor Islands (FBHI).*

This photo from the journal shows the beach and larger drumlin (or hill) on Great Brewster. Note the houses set back from the beach. For a view of Great Brewster Island in more modern times, see color section.

acres, and has a stone wharf, a bit of ancient ruin, and the summer-villa of the Hon. Benjamin Dean. A contented family lives on the island throughout the entire year." This family remains unidentified, but photos in the journal show other buildings on the island, and perhaps this refers to "William the Swede," the person who ferried the women to and from the island.

Elizabeth "Lizzie" Dean Adams, niece of Benjamin Dean Jr., thus had a connection to Great Brewster. Another connection was Merrie Tripper Helen Frances Ray French, who was the sister-in-law of Mary Ann French Dean, the wife of Benjamin Dean, owner of the island cottage. With the XV Club's interest in travel, the island loomed as a great adventure yet one that was not too distant. It was just challenging enough—note that if nine women made the original trip in 1879, only four opted to do so in 1891. Could the journal be a way of telling the others what they missed?

Today, Great Brewster is part of the Boston Harbor Islands National and State Park. (See chapter 7.)

5

IMPRESSIONS FROM THE GREAT
BREWSTER JOURNAL PHOTOGRAPHS

By Elizabeth Carella

*Elizabeth Carella is a photographic historian, experienced in working with an array
of early visual formats. She has served as photo curator and photographer for the
Harvard Semitic Museum and the Archives for Historical Documentation and worked
in collections throughout Europe, the Middle East and India. Exploring the Brewster
photographs for content and significance has afforded her a fresh opportunity to view rare
visions of Boston Harbor through the medium of the snapshot.*

One of the striking aspects of the Great Brewster journal is its adroit use
of photographs that document the trip. The photographer(s) used a
new technology, one that had been in use for only three years, that of
the "snapshot" camera. With this camera, the women managed to make a
visual recording of what they were seeing. With thorough precision, they
recorded the landscape, the house and—to a certain extent—each other.
Furthermore, they placed the photos into the journal with great care.

When, in 1888, George Eastman introduced the handheld "box camera"
known as the Kodak, formal studio portraiture and carefully composed
landscapes gave way to a new, spontaneous, readily accessible method of
recording people, events and scenery. Roll film replaced heavy glass plates.
Amateurs were now able to capture moments in time, although lack of
experience with exposure, composition and the need for a steady hand
sometimes yielded less than satisfactory results.

Processing presented further challenges when amateurs were able to develop
and print their own pictures. Chemical stains, shifts in density and dark

HARPER'S MAGAZINE ADVERTISER.

A GIFT WORTH HAVING.

(Feminine Chorus) : Oh ! isn't it lovely !   I must have a Kodak !

Send to The Eastman Company, Rochester, N. Y., for a
copy of "Do I want a Camera," (illustrated) free by mail.

This engraving from 1891 is a graphic example of Kodak's advertisements aimed toward women at the advent of the snapshot era. Four elegantly attired women surround a Kodak box camera, admiring its loveliness. The caption beneath the image attributes the sentiment "I must have a Kodak" to the "Feminine Chorus." *Courtesy of the Martha Cooper Kodak Girl Collection.*

thumbprints in the corners of photos resulted in smudges and uneven areas on the print. Scratches and flaws from the original negative also became visible in the final print. That print would then be affixed with glue to an album, the pages of which contained acids. That glue and those pages hastened the fading and deterioration of the prints, especially those prints that may not have been sufficiently washed after development. Additionally, in the case of the Brewster photos, some of the prints in the album were "retouched" with dark ink in an unsuccessful effort to fill in tears and holes in the photo paper.

For the Brewster Island journal, two types of cameras were used. The round images were made with one of the earliest Kodak box cameras, the Kodak No. 2. The images tend to be sharp and well exposed. They were professionally processed and have survived with very little fading. The camera, at a cost of $25 (about $700 today), came loaded with film that could yield up to one hundred exposures. That camera would then be sent to Kodak for development and printing and would be returned to the owner reloaded, all for an additional $10. The company's marketing slogan aimed at "Kodakers" was "You press the button and we do the rest." Many advertisements were directed at women.

The rectangular photographs in the journal were likely made using another early Kodak, the No. 3 from 1890 or, possibly, the Model A Daylight Kodak. The latter, introduced in 1891, could be loaded in subdued daylight. In the Great Brewster rectangular format photos, we find a range of subjects, including sweeping views of the island, the seawall and Bug Light. There are also more personal images recording the women as they sat on the porch reading, sewing and relaxing. The women can be seen gathering driftwood, wading in the surf and lifting a barrel of food items from the well, what they called "ye refrigerator."

A pair of unusually clear photos from the early pages of the journal show different views of the "Ye Charming East Room," upstairs in the cottage. While rustic, the cottage seemed to be well appointed with furniture. This photo is another example of how the women were intent on documenting their trip.

The photos appear to have been taken by more than one person. Perhaps each of the women took turns with the camera in order to learn about the photographic process. However, it is likely that Helen Whittier took the most technically and stylistically successful of the photos. Helen belonged to the Lowell Camera Club and participated in a photo exhibition in November 1890. An article later that month in the *Boston Globe* notes that Helen A. Whittier had "a number of interesting sketches made with a Kodak" in the exhibition, adding that they had been "snapped" on the fly. The photos had been "skillfully finished and mounted with breezy sketchiness," and the exhibit was one of artistic excellence.

Among the Great Brewster images, "Ye Charming East Room" and "Ye Joyous Kitchen," as well as the portrait of "The Lady Brewster," display the vision of a more experienced photographer than do some of the distant views made on the island. The round photos taken from the steamer along the route reveal a certain expertise, a skilled eye and a steady hand.

That said, even the less technically precise images in the journal contain significant details regarding Great Brewster Island, its structures and topography. Moreover, the photos are an indication of the women's desire to document, with new technology, a two-week sojourn in a special locale in Boston Harbor, one they would recall as "Our beloved Brewster."

YE LOG OF YE SQUARE PARTIE AT YE GREAT BREWSTER IN YE PLEASANT MONTH OF JULY 1891

What follows is a transcription of the entire text of the Great Brewster journal, followed by explanatory notes. All but eight of the journal's full pages and nearly all the photographs are reproduced. For color reproductions of selected pages, please see the central section of this book. This chapter is divided according to the daily entries. The notes at the end of each entry are meant to put the entries into context and add to the understanding of the women and their lives, as well as the history and lore of the Boston Harbor Islands. Many pages of the journal contained only photos, and these were not given page numbers by the women. The exact text has been transcribed with just a smattering of interpolations [*sic*] added to indicate a grammar or spelling issue in the original. Not all the words in every entry could be deciphered.

The transcription process made it clear that there were four to five different styles of writing. Reviewing the entries systematically, team member Allison Andrews distinguished four handwriting styles. Details in the content led to reasonable guesses about who penned which pages. In addition, a uniform pattern of turn-taking for writing the daily entries emerged. This helped narrow down the identities of all the women.

These are the writers and the dates for their entries. Notice the cycle of taking turns in order.

Helen Whittier, The Scribe: July 15, 19, 23, 27, 31
Lizzie Dean Adams, The Aristocrat: July 16, 20, 24, 28

Bella Coburn, The Acrobat: July 17, 21, 25, 29
Helen Ray French, The Autocrat: July 18, 22, 26, 30

There is a fifth hand: a stylized or decorative lettering used for the opening pages and for the captions on photographs and illustrations throughout the journal. This is likely the work of Helen Whittier. The evidence for this conclusion begins with the watercolor on the last page of the journal, which contains two important elements: her signature and several lines in the decorative "fifth hand" lettering incorporated into the painting. This associates the decorative lettering with Whittier. And since that decorative style is also found inserted into the common script style of several journal entries, those dates can be attributed to Helen Whittier as well.

Helen Whittier, the Scribe, seems to be the project leader. The first and last entries are hers. Her decorative lettering appears frequently and visually unifies the entries, possibly indicating her involvement throughout the process of creating the journal. As you read the original pages, have a look at the handwriting.

The authors are grateful to the Schlesinger Library of the Radcliffe Institute for Advanced Study for permission to reproduce the journal images. All pages of the journal and the photos are courtesy of the Schlesinger Library.

WEDNESDAY, JULY 15, 1891

And thou, O Boston, Mistress of the Towns,
Whom the pleased Bay with am'rous arms surrounds
Wednesday, July 15
--1891--

The Autocrat of the Brewster, having issued her mandate, the Aristocrat, the Acrobat and the Scribe met her at Rowe's Wharf in Boston at 9:15 on Wednesday morning. Leaving a temperature of ninety-in-the-shade behind us we had a breezy sail down the Harbor on the Nantasket Boat, notwithstanding the fact that we were sandwiched between a picnic from Lowell and a picnic from Worcester which filled the boat to overflowing. Arriving at Pemberton Pier, we disembarked with our numerous and weighty parcels, which represented only our personal belongings, most of the household goods and groceries, having been taken down to the Brewster some days before.

"And thou, O Boston, Mistress of the Towns,
whom the pleased Bay with amorous arms,
Surrounds."

Wednesday, July 15,
——— 1891 ———

The Autocrat of the Brewster, having
issued her mandate, — the Aristocrat, the Acrobat
and the Scribe met her at Rowe's Wharf in
Boston at 9.15 on Wednesday Morning. Leaving a
temperature of ninety-in-the-shade behind us,
we had a breezy sail down the Harbor in
the Nantasket Boat, notwithstanding the fact that

The journey begins on July 15, with this entry labeled as page 1. Note that the photo is labeled 6. All the photos are given a number in the journal.

2

we were sandwiched between a picnic from Lowell and a picnic from Worcester, which filled the boat to overflowing. Arriving at Pemberton Pier we disembarked with our numerous and weighty parcels, which represented only our personal belongings, most of the household goods and groceries, having been taken down to the Brewster some days before.

The Autocrat had arranged that William the Swedish fisherman who occupies the Island should meet us at Pemberton in time to sail on the Ebb tide, before 12 o'clock – that being the most favorable time to get through Hull Gut.

But we found no William there, and we composed ourselves for a little patient waiting; we landed about 10.15 a.m. and about 12,30 were gratified to see the tardy William appear. In the meantime however, the breeze had been stiffening, until the waves were all crested with white-caps and we decided to wait a little longer before embarking for the Great Brewster as we should undoubtedly get drenched while such a sea was on.

We therefore resigned ourselves to a longer wait and assuaged the pangs of hunger by making serious inroads on the corn-beef and bread

This is page 2 of the journal that describes the Trippers' journey to Great Brewster.

The Autocrat had arranged that William the Swedish fisherman who occupies the Island should meet us at Pemberton in time to sail on the ebb tide, before 12 o'clock, that being the most favorable time to get through Hull Gut.

But we found no William there, and composed ourselves for a little patient waiting; we landed about 10.15 A.M. and about 12.30 were gratified to see the tardy William appear. In the meantime however, the breeze had been stiffening until the waves were all crested with white-caps and we decided to wait a little longer before embarking for the Great Brewster, as we should undoubtedly get drenched while such a sea was on.

We therefore resigned ourselves to a longer wait and assuaged the pangs of hunger by making serious inroads on the corn-beef and bread which the Acrobat had smuggled in with her [wardrobe].

Pemberton Pier is not the worst place in the world to spend a summer day—and we felt grateful for the cool breeze, so refreshing after the many hot days we had endured at home. Comfortably seated on the shaded Pier, we read aloud from "The Social Departure," the title seeming not inappropriate to our present circumstances. At last William informed us that the wind had subsided a little and if we did not mind a slight wetting, he thought we had better start. Availing ourselves of the seclusion of the Toilet Room, we exchanged our worldly attire for the more primitive garb of the Brewster, and after much packing and stowing away of our impedimenta in the neat little "Lobster Rig," we set sail on a tempestuous sea. But the sun was bright overhead and soon we were safely out of the eddies of Hull Gut, and taking in only one or two small seas were quickly transported past the familiar Bug Light, and in forty-five minutes from the start landed on the Pier at the Great Brewster, in good condition. Our six hours wait on Hull Pier vanished from our minds as we trod once more the dear old Island which for two weeks is to be our home.

Arriving about 5 P.M. the Square Partie at once attacked the problem of setting up housekeeping, getting supper, and cleaning house before bedtime. The Autocrat and the Aristocrat undertook the cuisine, while the Acrobat and the Scribe wielded brooms and dustpans and at 7:30 P.M. a tired but triumphant quartette [sic] sat down to the tea table, graced with Nasturtiums brought from Mr. Dean's garden.

Menu—Wednesday July 15
Cold Corn Beef
Bread and butter
Tea
Rochester Jelly Cake
Cheese

Top: This photo is labeled "Landing at Pemberton Pier at Hull" and was taken during the trip to Great Brewster. Pemberton Pier was a bustling hub of activities as both a steamship landing and the terminus of the Nantasket branch of the Old Colony Railroad. The luxurious Hotel Pemberton was across the street from the pier, a convenient location for travelers.

Bottom: This photo is labeled "On Ye Nantasket Steamer." According to the 1888 *Kings Handbook of Boston Harbor*, "The Sail Down the Harbor: The perfection of physical comfort is enjoyed when, on a warm day of summer, one leaves the hot and crowded streets and many cares of the city and passes down Boston Harbor on one of its luxurious excursion-steamboats."

3

which the Acrobat had smuggled in with her
wardrobe.

Pemberton Pier is not the worst place in the
world to spend a summer day— and we felt
grateful for the cool breeze, so refreshing after the
many hot days we had endured at home.

Comfortably seated on the shaded
Pier, we read aloud from "The Social Departure",
the title seeming not inappropriate to our present
circumstances. — At last William informed us
that the wind had subsided a little and if we
did not mind a slight wetting, he thought we
had better start. Availing ourselves of the seclusion
of the Toilet Room, we exchanged our worldly attire
for the more primitive garb of the Brewster, and
after much packing and stowing away of our
impedimenta in the neat little "Sabota Rig", we

This page of the journal features a photo taken at Pemberton Pier, where the women waited
for "William the Swede" to appear to take them to Great Brewster.

4

set sail on a tempestuous sea. But the sun was bright overhead, and soon we were safely out of the eddies of Hull Gut, and taking in only one or two small seas were quickly transported past the familiar Bug Light, and in forty five minutes from the start, landed on the Pier at the Great Brewster, in good condition. Our six hours wait on Hull Pier vanished from our minds, as we trod once more the dear old Island which for two weeks is to be our home.

"Our dream was of an Island place
which distant seas made lonely; ——
A little Island, on whose face
The stars are watchers only."

Page 4 of the journal continues to describe their journey to the island with this photo and a quote from a poem by Elizabeth Barrett Browning. This photo was taken much later in the trip. For a modern view of the sandspit from Great Brewster, see the color section.

This satisfactory meal being despatched [*sic*] with the accompanying dishwashing, we sat for a while on the broad piazza watching the flash of the Boston Light which is our next door neighbor, while a gentle shower pattered over our heads. At 9:00 [?] P.M. we went upstairs. The Aristocrat and the Scribe were assigned to the East Room, known in 1879 as the

Hospital Ward from its containing at that time so many inmates. Now there are two double beds, and although the Autocrat intended to occupy the West Room and the Acrobat the next room, they finally camped down in the unoccupied bed in the East Room with the others. Then followed of course, much cheerful discourse such as XVs are wont to hold when evening shades prevail. To see the Autocrat sit up in bed with lighted candle in hand, to read aloud from King's Handbook:

> *"When the poor sailor, wet and cold,*
> *And with fatigue opprest,*
> *This happy island doth behold,*
> *He happy feels and blest,"* –

was a sight worthy of the palmiest days of the Brewster.

At last, to the soft patter of the rain upon the shingles over our head, we one by one went off with a more or less troubled slumber, with an occasional fog-horn accompaniment.

NOTES ON JULY 15

In this breezy first entry, the four women make their way from Lowell and Boston to Great Brewster Island by way of Rowes (formerly Rowe's) Wharf in Boston and Pemberton Point in Hull, clean up the house, have dinner and talk well into the night.

The personalities of the Merrie Trippers start to emerge in this first entry. The Autocrat of the Brewster "mandates" that the other women make this trip. The use of the word *Autocrat* is perhaps the most curious of the nicknames; it may be a reference to the popular *The Autocrat of the Breakfast-table*, a collection of essays published in 1858 by Oliver Wendell Holmes Sr., in which he refers to Boston's gold-domed State House as the "hub of the solar system," which tagged Boston with "The Hub" as a nickname. Holmes, a physician, poet, inventor and father of a future Supreme Court justice, was perhaps the epitome of the Boston intellectual elite. The women would later describe being able to see the gold-topped Massachusetts State House from the island.

The women apparently met at Rowes (formerly Rowe's) Wharf, a major working wharf of the Boston waterfront, to catch the Nantasket boat to Hull

5

Arriving about 5 P.M. the Square Party at once attacked the problem of setting up housekeeping, getting supper, and cleaning house before bedtime. The Autocrat and the Aristocrat undertook the cuisine, while the Acrobat and the Scribe wielded brooms and dustpans and at 7.30 P.M. a tired but triumphant quartette sat down to the tea table, graced with Nasturtiums brought from Mr. Dean's garden.

Menu — Wednesday July 15 —

Cold Corn-beef

Bread and butter

Tea —

Rochester Jelly Cake —

Cheese —

This satisfactory meal being despatched, with the accompanying dishwashing, we sat for a while on the broad piazza watching the flash of the Boston Light which is our next door neighbor, while a gentle shower pattered over our heads. At 9.30 P.M. we went up stairs. The Aristocrat and the Scribe were assigned

Page 5 of the journal begins the practice of recording the meals of the day. See the recipe for Rochester jelly cake in the notes that follow this entry.

6

to the East Room, known in 1879 as the Hospital Ward
from its containing at that time so many inmates.
Now there are two double beds, and although the
Autocrat intended to occupy the West Room and the
Associate the next room, they finally camped down
in the unoccupied bed in the East Room with the
others. Then followed of course, much cheerful discourse
such as ⚥'s are wont to hold when evening
shades prevail. To see the Autocrat sit up in bed
with lighted candle in hand, to read aloud from
King's Handbook

"When the poor sailor, wet and cold,
and with fatigue opprest,
This happy island doth behold,
He happy feels and blest,"—
was a sight

worthy of the palmiest days of the Brewster.
At last, to the soft patter of the rain upon the
shingles over our head, one one by one went off
into a more or less troubled slumber, with an
occasional fog-horn accompaniment.

The end of the first day of the adventure features a tiny illustration of a candle, likely a main source of light for the women. When was this illustration added? It is difficult to determine if this entry was done on the island or added later.

for the first step in their journey to the island. In 1764, John Rowe bought the land and built the first Rowes Wharf, which extended a short distance into Boston Harbor. It was used for commercial shipping. Today, the Boston Harbor Hotel is located on Rowes Wharf, where the Harborwalk affords an expansive view of the harbor.

The Pemberton, Nantasket and Hingham steamers were a common and convenient way to get from Boston (departing from Rowes Wharf) to either Hingham or the town of Hull, part of which was known as Nantasket ("Land of the Changing Tides"). From there, passengers could spend the day or days either on the Hull peninsula or in Hingham in one of the many palatial hotels. Hull became a tourist resort in 1825, and by 1840, steamboats were making three trips a day. The Old Colony Railroad established a Nantasket Beach branch that had twelve stops. The end of the line was Pemberton Pier, the location of the grand Hotel Pemberton.

The July 15 entry begins with a few lines of poetry, the first of what would be many such citations. The selection is from a longer piece written by Mather Byles in 1728, according to *King's Handbook of Boston Harbor*, which includes the entire stanza on page 153:

And thou, O Boston, Mistress of the Towns,
Whom the pleas'd Bay with am'rous arms surrounds
Let thy warm transports blaze in num'rous fires,
And beaming Glories glitter on thy spires.

Indeed, the Trippers frequently cite *King's Handbook of Boston Harbor*, which was written by M.F. Sweetser and published in 1882 by the Moses King Corporation, a well-known publisher of travel guidebooks. *King's Handbook of Boston Harbor* was a comprehensive account of the cities, towns, land and islands that were part of the Boston Harbor of the late 1800s. Both a travel log and historical account, the book provided a cultural perspective of the times, the people and the environment. A laudatory review in the *Boston Globe* of August 13, 1882, declared it should be dignified by a name better than "handbook," as it was "a studious and conscientious history" with more than two hundred illustrations. Its publication also perhaps represented the evolution of the islands from a working part of the city to more of a tourism destination. A third edition of the handbook was published in 1889. The Friends of the Boston Harbor Islands republished *King's Handbook* in 1988 and again in 2016 to bring its descriptions, information and insights to a new generation.

This photo is accompanied by a quote from *Childe Harold's Pilgrimage* by Lord Byron: "Pass we the long unvarying course, the track / Oft trod, that never leaves a trace behind."

The women were obliged to wait at the Pemberton Pier for the arrival of "William the Swedish fisherman" who apparently lived on Great Brewster. He is not otherwise identified. However, many fisherfolk did live on the Harbor Islands, most notably a community of Portuguese immigrants on Long Island. When forced to leave Long Island when it was taken over by the City of Boston for social services, many of the Portuguese floated their small houses to Peddocks Island, where they established a community and continued to ply their fishing trade. Today, a few of the original cottages, some owned by the descendants, remain on Peddocks Island.

William did not, it seems, live in the house that the women were to occupy on Great Brewster, and there are photos of other, smaller structures on the island where he may have resided.

During their wait, the women indulged their habit of reading out loud to one another, perhaps the way a future generation would hover over

This photo shows the "piazza" of the house with a prominent American flag, which would have had forty-three stars. The forty-three-star flag became official on July 4, 1890.

their mobile phones. In this case, they were reading *A Social Departure: How Orthodocia and I Went Round the World by Ourselves*, written by popular Canadian author Sara Jeannette Duncan in 1890. This international bestseller was based on a series of newspaper articles Duncan wrote about her trip around the world in the latter part of the nineteenth century. Duncan (1861–1922) was a bestselling author of her era in both fiction and nonfiction (she authored more than twenty books) but is rarely read today. She was a pioneer in travel writing by women. On January 25, 1890, Nellie Bly, an investigative journalist for the *New York World*, completed her effort to match the challenge in Jules Verne's popular novel *Around the World in 80 Days*. Traveling solo, Nellie completed the trip in seventy-two days. The four women surely knew

This photo shows the house on Great Brewster from a romantic angle. It is accompanied by a quote, "We may build more splendid habitations, But we cannot buy with gold the old associations," which is from "The Golden Milestone" by Henry Wadsworth Longfellow. The full quotation is "We may build more splendid habitations / Fill our rooms with paintings and with sculptures / But we cannot / Buy with gold the old associations!"

about this feat and later said they found Duncan's book "amusing." Perhaps it also planted a seed of ambition in Helen Whittier, who would spend the last part of her life traveling extensively. They also used the wait to take photographs of the activity at Pemberton Pier.

When William did make his appearance, the women rushed to change their clothes from their "worldly attire for the more primitive garb of the Brewster." Women, particularly wealthy women, were obliged to dress formally any time they were in public. What the modern reader immediately notices is that the "casual" or "primitive" garb of the women—long skirts, jackets and hats—seems rather formal to modern eyes.

It's noteworthy that this chapter contains photos that seem to be taken from aboard a ship, which requires a steady hand. These photos are accompanied by bits of poetry; one quote is from *Childe Harold's Pilgrimage* by Lord Byron (whom they quote a lot): "Pass we the long unvarying course, the track/Oft trod, that never leaves a trace behind." The poem continues:

> *Pass we the calm, the gale, the change, the tack,*
> *And each well-known caprice of wave and wind;*
> *Pass we the joys and sorrows sailors find,*
> *Coop'd in their winged sea-girt citadel;*
> *The foul, the fair, the contrary, the kind,*
> *As breezes rise and fall and billows swell,*
> *Till on some jocund morn—lo, land! and all is well.*

When the women finally arrive on the island, they write of being able to "trod once more the dear old Island which for two weeks is to be our home," another indication that this was a return trip. The landscape photo included in this section is significant. It was taken from the long Great Brewster spit, looking back on the island. Perhaps fittingly, the photo is illustrated with a poem called "An Island'" by Elizabeth Barrett Browning, which reads:

> *My dream is of an island-place*
> *Which distant seas keep lonely,*
> *A little island on whose face*
> *The stars are watchers only.*

The pages of this entry are filled with photographs and quotations. This entry contains the *Plan of House at the Great Brewster* (see page 19) as well as photographs that seem aimed at documenting the house, its rooms and the landscape (see pages 53, 62, 68, 69, 72).

An article in the 1893 *Boston Globe* on the XV Club makes reference to a trip by nine members to Great Brewster Island in which they established "cooperative housekeeping," and the four women certainly showed this by dividing up the tasks of cleaning and cooking almost as soon as they arrive. They also graced their table with a bouquet of nasturtiums that came from "Mr. Dean's garden." This would perhaps mean that Benjamin Dean, the lawyer and politician and uncle of Lizzie Dean Adams who leased Great Brewster, spent some time working on the landscape around the house.

This section also has the first recording of an important activity: the meals. They finish off the corned beef with bread and butter, tea, cheese and a Rochester jelly cake. What is a Rochester jelly cake? We found a version on the internet roughly contemporary with the Great Brewster trip. Like many recipes of the time, it does not give a baking temperature or time.

Rochester Jelly Cake
One and one-half cups sugar, two eggs, one-half cup butter, three-fourths cup milk, two heaping cups flour with one teaspoonful cream of tartar, one-half teaspoonful of soda, dissolved in the milk. Put half the above mixture in a small shallow tin, and to the remainder add one teaspoonful molasses, one-half cup raisins (chopped) or currants, one-half teaspoonful cinnamon, cloves, allspice, a little nutmeg and one tablespoonful flour. Bake this in same kind of tins. Put the sheets of cake together, while warm, with jelly between.

Temperature control was difficult in a wood-burning stove. The amount of heat generated varied as the wood burned. This required a lot of attention from people working in the kitchen, who had to employ various observations to get some idea of how hot the oven was, sometimes cooking while the oven cooled. Depending on the availability of gas or electricity, some people had gas or electric ovens, but the thermostat was not invented until early in the twentieth century. For more, see *Food Crumbles'* "The History of the Oven—A Timeline" at foodcrumbles.com. Given the difficulty of baking on the island, it is likely they brought an already-baked cake with them. But if you want to make this delicious cake (as did one of our researchers), bake it at 350 degrees for about thirty minutes.

Why did the women keep such meticulous track of their food consumption? They may have been in the habit of writing menus for the cooks or servants they employed. Harvard professor John Stilgoe suggests that the women were actually reveling in the chance to cook for only themselves, not a household. "They were on vacation not only from their families but from their servants," he said in an interview with project editor Stephanie Schorow in January 2009. As one of the research team noted, food is always a major part of any women's retreat or camping trip today (see the epilogue), so perhaps this should not be considered unusual.

This photo is described as "Ye Sumptuous Dining Room with a peep into ye Kitchen." A bit of irony is at play here, yet the dining room seems well-stocked with china and other serving dishes.

With documentary precision, this section of the journal includes photos of various rooms of the house, each labeled with seaworthy slang and poetry. They quote "Blest be that spot, where cheerful guests retire / To pause from toil, and time their evening fire!" from the long poem "The Traveller" by Oliver Goldsmith. To photos of the house itself, they add: "We may build more splendid habitations / But we cannot buy with gold the old associations," which is from "The Golden Mile-Stone" by Henry Wadsworth Longfellow.

The quartet finished their day by listening to the Autocrat read out loud from *King's Handbook* while seated in bed and holding a candle, which amused the author of this entry no end. She includes a quick sketch of a candle to conclude the entry. The writer of this entry is likely Helen Whittier.

Thursday, July 16, 1891

In the early dawn the Autocrat is seen to disappear from the East Room with pillow in hand to find more comfortable quarters for a morning nap. The Acrobat soon joins her and they together prepare the first breakfast of Oat Meal – Corn-beef – Baked potatoes – Toast – coffee and tea. The table was graced with nasturtiums. The Scribe takes to the task of sweeping the piazza while the others make the Kitchen orderly, lower the meat, butter, and milk into the well and attend to the bleaching on the grass.

The beds are made and then the Square Partie repair to the piazza to listen to the reading by the Scribe of the Journal of '79. Lunch today was served in the Kitchen. Lobsters, crackers, Orange Marmalade, Ginger Snaps and Cheese after which the Autocrat and Scribe write in the vestibule while the others gather clover blossoms for a [indecipherable] to be served later—In their wanderings they interview a man from among those working on the wall to ask if he will take letters to Fort Warren to mail. This opens a way for sending daily letters to the city.

Our meals come surprisingly near together [;] dinner tonight consisted of Cold tongue – boiled potatoes – bread – Orange Marmalade – Cake – Cocoa-nut Cakes Maccaroons [sic] and Tea. The appetites are all good and everything is perfectly delicious – After dinner we go out to the wall to see the work going on there – The winter storms have thrown up much of the stone work and the men are replacing the stones. We sat on the wall watching the beautiful clouds - the evening light in the Light House, and the steamers proceeding to sea –

The Autocrat read aloud from *Kenilworth* – Altogether it had been a most perfect summer day and night – We sat late on the piazza with the moon shining bright and watched the Excursion steamers pass – and before retiring listen to more from our book in the dining room – The never failing driftwood gives us ample exercise in fetching it for the kitchen stove –

Notes on July 16

This was another perfect day for the Trippers of relaxation, meals and reading from *Kenilworth*, a historical romance novel set in Elizabethan England written by Sir Walter Scott and published in 1821.

This entry appears to be in a different handwriting; note the use of dashes for periods. Also note the placement of two small but exquisite watercolors

7

Thursday
July 16, 1891

In the early dawn the Autocrat is seen to disappear from the East Room with pillow in hand to find more comfortable quarters for a morning nap. The Acrobat soon joins her and they together prepare the first breakfast of Oat Meal - Corned beef - Baked potatoes - Toast - coffee & tea. The table was graced with nasturtiums. The Scribe takes to the task of sweeping the piazza while the others make the Kitchen orderly. Lower the meat, butter and milk into the well and attend to the Heaching on the grass - The beds are made and then the Square Partie repair to the piazza to listen to the reading by the Scribe of the Journal of '79 - Lunch today was served in the Kitchen - Lobsters, crackers, Orange Marmalade, Ginger Snaps and, Cheese. After which the Autocrat and Scribe write in the Notebook while the others

This is the first page of the entry for July 16. This entry is filled with watercolor illustrations with the initials B.C. Pages 8 and 9 of the journal for July 16 are reproduced in the color section of this book.

This photo in the journal shows one of the women at the well and is captioned "Ye Aristocrat and Ye Refrigerator." The women used the well as a temporary refrigerator for food storage until the delivery of ice for the ice chest.

and a pen-and-ink drawing of a four-leaf clover in the text by B.C. '91 ("Ye Artistic Acrobat" or Bella Coburn).

The Scribe reads from the "Journal of 1879," confirming that this is a return visit to Great Brewster. If the *Boston Globe* story on the XV Club is accurate, then nine of the women made that previous trip. It also means that perhaps there is another Great Brewster journal out there. (Perhaps this book will bring someone forward to produce that volume.)

The women also make great use of a well on the island to keep their food cool—later they would get ice for an ice chest. Of great delight to the women is the chance to have their daily mail delivered by the men working on the seawall to Fort Warren and hence to Boston. In other words, they are not so different from those of us who vow to turn off phones and laptops on our vacations but can't resist sending text or emails.

As for the red clover, the women may have been making a kind of tea. Tea made by steeping red clover (*Trifolium pratense*) blossoms in simmering water was a popular, slightly sweet drink with some medicinal properties that would likely have been known to the women.

A few curiosities: If this is the first full day of vacation, what are they bleaching on the lawn and why? The photo of "the business end" of the house included in chapter 1 shows white patches on the lawn. Could these be rags that were used in the cleaning? Or are these undergarments that need regular washing? Or another kind of laundry?

FRIDAY, JULY 17, 1891

This is Acrobatic Verse:

In our eastern chamber casement,
Early peeps (or glares) the sun;
And our bird, a meadow lark,
Sings his sweet little song.

Though our beds are rough we sleep well, Morning comes too soon. Every moment is good; night or day.
For breakfast we had:
   Oat Meal, Hash, Buttered Toast, tea and coffee
   "The table was graced with Nasturtiums." the same ones.

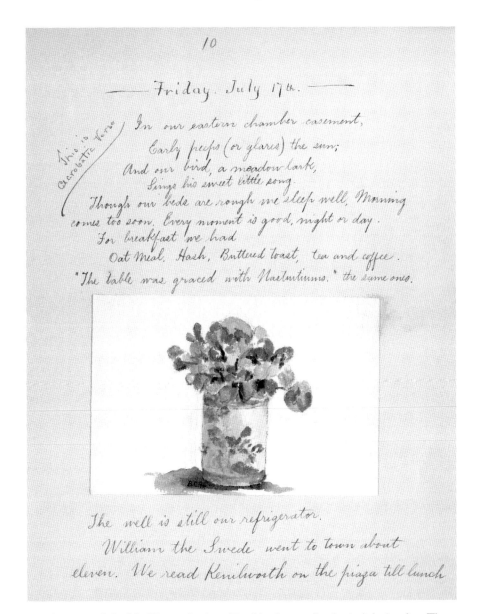

10

——— Friday. July 17th. ———

This is Acrobatic Verse

In our eastern chamber casement,
    Early peeps (or glares) the sun;
And our bird, a meadow-lark,
    Sings his sweet little song.
Though our beds are rough we sleep well, Morning
comes too soon. Every moment is good, night or day.
    For breakfast we had
    Oat Meal, Hash, Buttered toast, tea and coffee.
"The table was graced with Nasturtiums." the same ones.

The well is still our refrigerator.
William the Swede went to town about
eleven. We read Kenilworth on the piaza till lunch

The first page of the July 17 entry begins with a bit of poetry by the Artistic Acrobat. Thus, we suspect this was written by Bella Coburn. One of her watercolors is included on this page. To see this page in color, go to the color midsection.

The well is still our refrigerator.

William the Swede went to town about eleven.

We read Kenilworth on the piaza [*sic*] till lunch

12.30 – Crackers & milk, cheese, quince sauce, cake etc.

Afternoon we sewed, wrote, sketched, & photographed.

About five o'clock the Aristocrat & the Acrobat gathered our daily fuel, and carried the letters for mailing to the government workmen.

The nasturtiums again decorate the dinner table, and we had cold tongue, potatoes, tomatoes, & mince pie. After arranging the house we walked on the sea wall towards Middle Brewster, and read aloud there till the mosquitoes drove us home. Sat on the piazza in the moonlight till ten, then played Reversi in the dining room till eleven.

One boat gone to town, the other up for repairs.

No milk to-night.

NOTES ON JULY 17

This short entry focuses on detailing food and activity. The beginning "Acrobatic Verse" might imply that this entry was written by Bella Coburn or "Ye Artistic Acrobat." Her initials are on the lovely little illustration of the nasturtiums from "Mr. Dean's garden," which have been delighting the women.

A few key details can be extracted from this entry. First, the women revel in calling the outside deck "the piazza," something that today might be called a front or back porch. The chief source of fuel seems to be driftwood that is gathered to burn in the stove or perhaps a fireplace. The reference to "milk" is interesting. While the women are clearly in a remote place, they are not beyond the reach of commerce, as they seem to rely on William to get milk and other supplies and on the workmen to deliver their letters.

Photo 19 of three of the women on the piazza gives a sense of their contentment. One is likely sewing some kind of embroidery; it's noteworthy that they are performing particularly womanly activities of the day. This photo is inserted into the copy, so if this entry was written on-site, space had to be left for a photo that was presumed to be forthcoming. For the first page of this entry with nasturtium watercolor in full color, see color midsection insert.

11.

12.30— Crackers & milk, cheese, quince sauce, cake &c.
Afternoon we sewed, wrote, sketched, & photographed.

—19

About five o'clock the Aristocrat & the Acrobat
gathered our daily fuel, and carried the letters
for mailing to the government workmen.
The nasturtiums again decorate the dinner table,
and we had cold tongue, potatoes, tomatoes, & mince pie.
After arranging the house we walked on the
sea wall towards Middle Brewster, and read
aloud there till the mosquitoes drove us home.
Sat on the piazza in the moonlight till ten, then
played Reversi in the dining room till eleven.
One boat gone to town, the other up for repairs.
No milk to night.

Page 11 of the journal keeps up the habit of listing the day's meals. The photo shows three
of the women reading or drawing and sewing on the piazza, with long skirts and hats.

Quince is a fruit with similarities to both apples and pears. It can be quite sour, so it's often made into a sauce or jam. Reversi, invented in 1883, is a board game for two players and a precursor to the game Othello, which was patented in 1971.

The temperature deep inside the well would have been in the mid-fifty-degree range year-round, so, during the summer months, the temperature inside the well would have been around fifteen to twenty degrees cooler than that at the surface.

Bella Coburn's artistry—and that of the other women—was likely affected by the trends in painting and art in the mid- to late 1800s that began to flourish. This may be driven by a number of factors. In 1870, legislation was passed in Massachusetts to mandate that drawing be taught in all public schools. In addition, free drawing classes would be provided for men, women and children in communities with populations over ten thousand. Using the mind in different ways was beginning to be valued and was one of the many reasons the legislation was passed. The skill of drawing also became a finishing touch for women to have in certain social circles. Also, in 1871 the Massachusetts Board of Education created a traveling museum. The museum brought visual art to local communities by horse-drawn carriages. In 1873, the Massachusetts Normal Art School (now the Massachusetts College of Art and Design) was opened in response to great public interest in drawing education. It was the first freestanding visual arts school in the United States.

Women did not have many opportunities to formally develop their art skills or make a career in the arts. A number of women moved or traveled to Europe, where there was more acceptance and opportunity. These included artists like Mary Cassatt, Cecilia Beaux, Elizabeth Nourse and Edmonia Lewis.

This entry likely was written by Bella Coburn, the Artistic Acrobat, and Helen Whittier added the note at the top indicating "Acrobatic verse."

SATURDAY, JULY 18, 1891

To be awakened at 6:30 this morning by a burst of melody informing me that the
   "Morning light is breaking
   and darkness disappears"
was not altogether satisfactory especially as I would have known directly, I did awaken naturally that such was the case. But I dressed and descended and

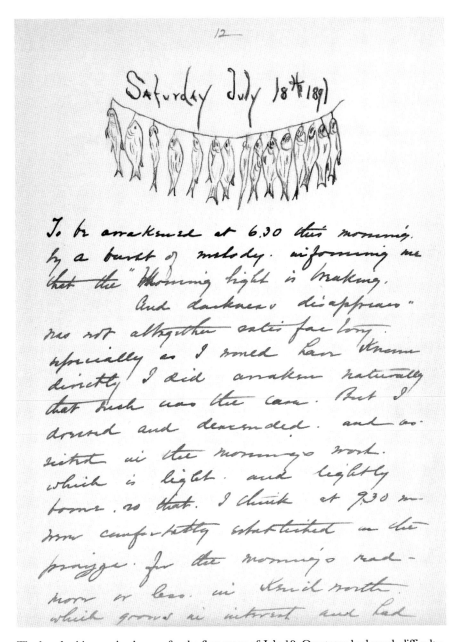

The handwriting again changes for the first entry of July 18. Our team had much difficulty in deciphering this style. The author was prolific, and it raises the question if this particular entry was produced on-site, although photos do break up this text.

13

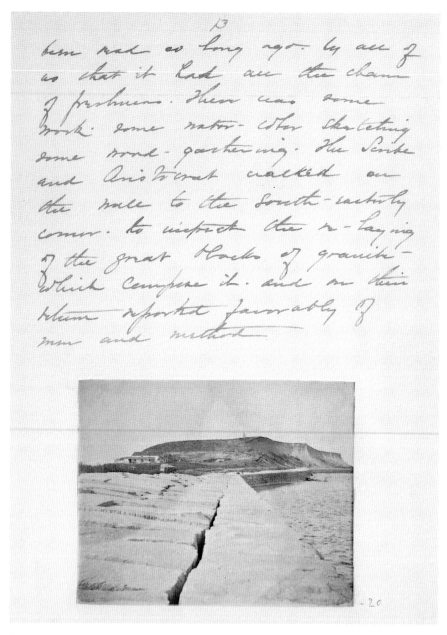

The second page of July 18 features a photo that captures the sweeping landscape of Great Brewster. A team of stonemasons from Boston is working on the seawall, although we don't see any workmen in these photos. The erosion on the side of the northern drumlin is quite obvious here.

assisted in the morning's work which is light and lightly borne so that I think at 9:30 we were comfortably established on the piazza for the morning's read – more or less in Kenilworth which grows in interest and had been read so long ago by all of us that it had all the charm of freshness. Then was some work, some water-color sketching, some wood-gathering. The Scribe and Aristocrat walked on the wall to the south-easterly corner to inspect the re-laying of the great blocks of granite – which compose it and on their return reported favorably of men and method.

Meantime we who remained behind prepared luncheon, serving it contrary to preceding custom on the round table in the vestibule using for the first time, a white cloth presented by Mrs. Partridge and also for the last time the nasturtiums gathered in the Dean garden early Wednesday A.M. last and surviving the long days exposure to heat and looking well until now. Later more work, letters, this log, rested.

The day grows gray and cloudy with light dashes of rain so it was thought prudent to get more wood to be well supplied in case of prolonged storm. At noon William appeared bringing the much desired ice and the first mail as now we no longer have to fetch and carry to the well all our perishable food, milk, butter, meat. After dinner we sat for a time in the dark watching the fog gather and the lights – disappear. The fog came and went and came again but after the evening given to "Halma" and to Kenilworth and as we made ready for the night, the lights of Boston and the down-reaching coast now plainly visible. It was later, eleven or eleven and a half when we went upstairs. During the night there were several severe but short rains which pelted on the near roof like pebbles. At 1 [or 11] P.M. the thermometer recorded seventy-two degrees.

Saturday July 18th, 1891
Breakfast–
Baked potatoes
Coffee – Bacon – Tea
Dry toast
Luncheon
Cold tongue
Milk. Bread and butter
Cake, marmalade
Dinner
Boiled potatoes
Cod-fish – Egg sauce
Mince pie
Tea

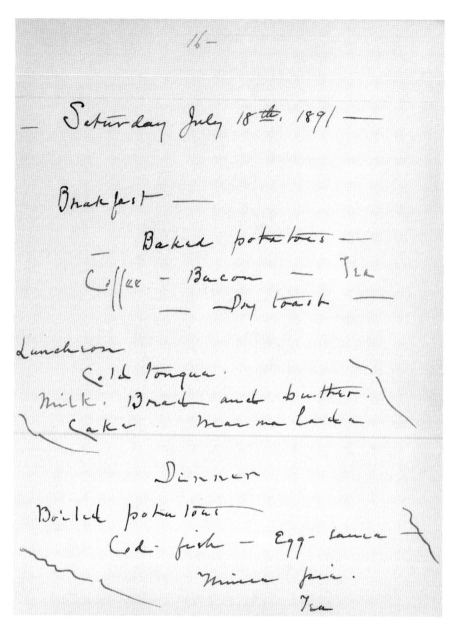

Page 16 of the journal repeats the date of Saturday, July 18 at the top and lists the menu of the day. It appears to have been written by a different hand, perhaps by one of the other Merrie Trippers who noticed that the day's menu had not been mentioned at the beginning of the entry and then made the necessary editorial adjustments.

NOTES ON JULY 18

Beginning with a sketch of a line with fish hanging from it and a quote from the "The Morning Light Is Breaking" (1832) by Samuel Francis Smith, this entry has a slightly different tone. The handwriting is dramatically different—and far less legible—and the author uses the first-person singular pronoun. Since there's a mention of the Scribe and the Aristocrat and the handwriting differs from the previous entry, which was likely by the Acrobat or Bella Coburn, this was likely written by the Autocrat, Helen Frances Ray French. If so, it would imply that she, as well as Whittier and Coburn, dabbled in drawing, although her work is less refined. This entry also differs from other entries in that the day's menu is listed at the end of the entry. "This log" is mentioned in the list of activities following lunch: "more work, letters, this log, rested." Obviously, something was being written on the island.

The women reference the game of Halma (Greek for "jump"), a checkers-type board game, invented about 1880, in which players attempt to move a number of pieces from one corner of a square board containing 256 squares to the opposite corner. There is a reference to a "Mrs. Partridge," but nothing else about who she is.

Whose singing voice (or was it a loud bird?) awakened this somewhat annoyed writer at 6:30 a.m.?

SUNDAY, JULY 19, 1891

Thermometer 74°
Wind S.W.
Breakfast 9:30 A.M.
Coffee – Oatmeal –
Fishballs – Salt Pork – Fried potatoes –
Toast
Lunch –
Lobster just boiled – Crackers
Preserved Ginger
Dinner 5 P.M.
Fricassee Chicken on Toast
Boiled Potatoes
Tea

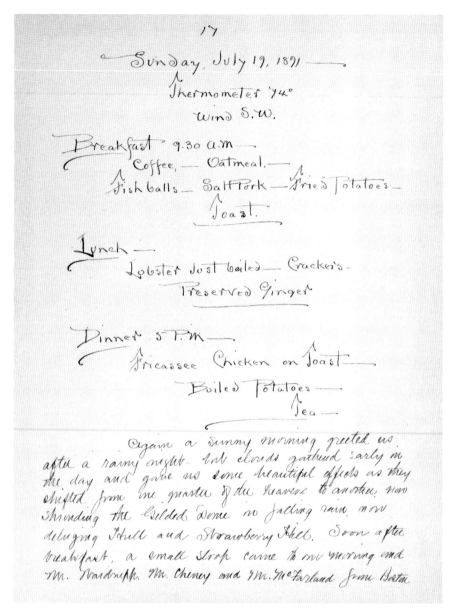

17

Sunday, July 19, 1891

Thermometer 74°

Wind S.W.

Breakfast 9.30 a.m
Coffee, — Oatmeal, —
Fish balls — Salt Pork — Fried Potatoes —
Toast.

Lunch —
Lobster Just boiled — Crackers —
Preserved Ginger

Dinner 5 P.M —
Fricassee Chicken on Toast —
Boiled Potatoes —
Tea —

Again a sunny morning greeted us.
after a rainy night — but clouds gathered early in
the day and gave us some beautiful effects as they
shifted from one quarter of the heavens to another, now
shrouding the Gilded Dome in falling rain, now
deluging Hull and Strawberry Hill. Soon after
breakfast, a small sloop came to our mooring and
Mr. Nardruph, Mr. Cheney and Mr. McFarland from Boston

Page 17 of the journal, the first page of the July 19 entry.

86

Again a sunny morning greeted us after a rainy night but clouds gathered early in the day and gave us some beautiful effects as they shifted from one quarter of the heavens to another, now shrouding the Gilded Dome in falling rain, now deluging Hull and Strawberry Hill. Soon after breakfast a small sloop came to our mooring and Mr. Wardrupp, Mr. Cheney, Mr. McFarland from Boston came ashore, bringing us the *Sunday Globe* and letters to the Autocrat and Acrobat.

The young men went down to William's "humble cat" and bought all his lobsters, built a fire on the beach and boiled them, bringing five up to us, and we had the pleasure of eating them hot for lunch. While Mr. Wardrupp [?] was chatting with us on the piazza one of the "local" showers came our way and great activity ensued on the part of the Acrobat who after rescuing the log and other important papers from a shower-bath, in the vestibule discovered several streams of water pouring through the roof of the East Room - which necessitated the use of all available crockery in catching the rain and the stripping and drying of all the Aristocrat's bedding. This episode was soon over however and benefitted us by giving us a tubful of soft water beside almost filling our water barrel. About 3 P.M. Mr. Wardrupp and his friends left us having taken our mail and some commissions for the larder. We then took up Kenilworth and read aloud till dinner time when we heartily enjoyed the Calf Island chicken which William brought to us with the milk last night.

After dinner instead of our usual walk, we sat on the piazza and enjoyed the beautiful sunset which filled the sky and water with glory, and when the moon almost at the full appeared from behind the fleecy clouds we felt that Nature had shown us many of her varying moods on this day. We sat in the moonlight till late discoursing as old friends will, then betook us to the dining room to read aloud a Sermon on Faithfulness, and then a half hour of Kenilworth finished our day.

NOTES ON JULY 19

Even on their rough island getaway, the women seem to be able to observe the social niceties of hosting guests. The visitors from Boston seem to be on the same social standing as the women, and interestingly, they bring a copy of the *Boston Globe*, one of the several newspapers of the city at the time.

18

came ashore, bringing us the Sunday Globe and letters
to the Autocrat and Acrobat. The young men went down
to Williams' humble cot and
brought all his lobsters,
built a fire on the beach
and boiled them, bringing
free up to us, and we
had the pleasure of eating
them hot for lunch.
While Mr. Woodnuff was
chatting with us on the
piazza one of the "local"
steamers came one way, and great activity ensued
on the part of the Acrobat who after rescuing
the Log and other important papers from a shower-
bath in the vestibule, discovered several streams
of water pouring through the roof of the East Room
which necessitated the use of all available crockery
in catching the rain, and the stripping and drying
of all the aristocrat's bedding. This episode was
soon over however and benefitted us by giving
us a tub-ful of soft water beside almost filling
our water barrel. About 3 P. M. Mr. Woodnuff and
his friends left us having taken our mail and
some commissions for the larder. We then took
up Kenilworth and read aloud till dinner time
when we heartily enjoyed the Calf Island chicken

Page 18 of the journal continues the entry for Sunday, July 19, and includes a photo of one of the other structures on the island. See page 19 of the journal, the last page of the July 19 entry, in the color section. The freshly cooked lobster in the illustration looks ready for butter.

This photo is labeled "Ye Jolly Postman" and seems to be a reference to the yachtsman who brought the women their mail.

Evidence suggests "Mr. Cheney" is Benjamin Pierce Cheney Jr. (1866–1942), the scion of a wealthy Boston family and a man famous in the lore of the Boston Harbor Islands. Cheney married the famous stage actress Julia Arthur in 1898. One summer, they rented a house on Middle Brewster Island from Augustus Russ, and when Russ declined to sell it to them, they built their own sumptuous summer home, The Moorings, on Calf Island in 1902. Calf Island is just offshore from Great Brewster, and some of the photos in the journal show structures on that island. Cheney's father, Benjamin Pierce Cheney Sr. (1815–1895), was a prominent businessman and would have been seventy-five at this time, so it is more likely the younger Cheney, then twenty-five, is the Mr. Cheney referenced.

The name of Wardrupp (sometimes spelled with one *p* or perhaps spelled Nardrupp or Wordrop) proved to be a challenge to identify. Researcher Suzanne Gall Marsh combed through two books about the Boston Yacht Club that listed club members over the years and found nothing close to this spelling. Researcher Martha Mayo identified a Civil War colonel David W. Wardrop (1824–1898), who was an inspector for the Custom House of Boston from 1870 to 1898. His son George William Wardrop (1857–1930) was working at 246 Federal Street at age thirty-three, according to the

1890 Boston city directory. So he was most likely "Wardrupp," who, with Benjamin Cheney Jr., was one of the "young men from Federal Street" who visited the Merrie Trippers on Brewster Island.

There is no McFarland listed in the Boston Yacht Club membership. Mayo found records for Edwin Stanley McFarland (1852–1900) in the 1890 Boston city directory. At age thirty-eight, he was superintendent, bonded warehouse, Custom House of Boston. This McFarland might have been the third young visitor to Great Brewster Island.

Incidentally, Cheney and his wife, Julia, enjoyed only a few summers at their Calf Island home, which fell into ruin in subsequent years. Today, only the remains of a chimney mark the site of The Moorings. Cheney, a one-time millionaire, suffered a reversal of fortune later in life and died in 1942 of thirst or exposure when he wandered from his car in an Arizona desert. Julia had a long acting career and died in 1950. She requested her ashes be buried at sea.

In another journal entry, the women enjoy "Calf Island chicken," which could mean someone kept chickens on the islands just as someone kept "The Lady Brewster," the cow, on Great Brewster.

This may be the boat that brought "Ye Jolly Postman" and others to the island, as it was matched with the photo of the Jolly Postman. It is captioned "Ye Merrie Yacht."

William's "humble cat" refers to a catboat, a particularly New England small boat innovation, which has a single sail and is often used for fishing. According to John Stilgoe, writing in *Alongshore,*

> *Unlike other New England firsts from schooner to clipper ships, catboats originated in the simplest of early nineteenth century Cape Cod and Narragansett Bay boat shops....Small-craft historians have argued since the 1920s that Yankee builders modified a colonial New Netherlands hull like the shoal-draft ones depicted in so many seventeenth-century Dutch oil paintings....By 1859 everyone from Salem South to Cape May, New Jersey knew the catboat as a distinct type.*

The origin of the name is mysterious, according to Stilgoe. It may reflect the concept of "turns quick like a cat," or "goes to windward like a cat." In the 1880s, writes Stilgoe, catboat fishermen began chartering their small craft to parties of summer visitors to islands off the coast or for sails in shallow-water bays.

MONDAY, JULY 20, 1891

Thermometer 74° A.M, 70° P.M.
Wind S.S.E.

Menu
Breakfast 8 A.M.
Coffee and Tea
Milk Toast – Bacon
Hashed Potatoes

Lunch – noon
Lobster
Olives, Marmalade and Quince
Crackers and Cheese

Dinner 5:30
Chicken Baked Potatoes
Maccaroni [*sic*] and cream
Toast and Tea
Assorted Cake

Above: The first page of the July 20 entry begins with the day's menu.

Opposite: Page 21 of the journal continues the July 20 entry and includes a photo of the cottage and a drumlin or hill on Great Brewster.

The Scribe and [one or me] prepared the breakfast today – and all helped in the morning work. Views were taken of the East Room, and later all resorted to the piazza to listen to the reading of Kenilworth.

After lunch the square partie went out to gather wood beyond the dock and brought a fine supply. We missed the men from the sea wall - they did not come from town. William went to the city and took our mail and commissions. Toward night the clouds looked threatening and after dinner as we sat on the piazza the fog came in and the foghorn commenced to blow and kept it up all night. We sat out as long as the dampness allowed and then went to the dining room to listen to Kenilworth which grows in interest. To bed at ten o'clock.

NOTES ON JULY 20

This entry, while short on details, adds to our understanding of the sojourn. The writer refers to "the Scribe" and either "me" or "one," so we suspect Whittier was not the writer. The writer also references photos taken of the East Room—those photographs appear earlier in the journal. Looking at the slight overlap of the photo numbered 27 on the journal page 21 and the lack of a caption, it may be that this was written on the island and space was left for a potential photo.

Lobster was again on the menu—this time for lunch—and the women didn't seem to stint on dessert. They also continue the reading out loud of *Kenilworth*.

The photos in this entry are particularly evocative. They include a photo labeled "Gathering driftwood at Great Brewster" that shows two women in hats carrying a basket between them on the beach, the hill behind them. It is paired with a quote: "They fetch their sea-born treasures home," which is a paraphrase from the poem "Each and All" by Ralph Waldo Emerson: "I fetched my sea-born treasures home…"

The entry includes a photo of all four women together. In fact, there may be five people in this photo—it's difficult to determine. Posing with a basket, they are shown seated, standing and lying down, the hill behind them. We can easily identify where this spot is today on Great Brewster; it's on the west side of the island on the shore. What is curious is: Who took the photo? It is rather out of focus, which suggests the photographer was not Whittier or another of the women. It is accompanied by an extended quote:

> *How very silent is the sea tonight!*
> *The little waves climb up the shore and lay*
> *Cool cheeks upon the ever-moving sands*
> *That follow swift their whispering retreat.*
> *I would I knew what things their busy tongues,*
> *Confess to Earth.*

This photo, labeled "Gathering driftwood at Great Brewster," shows two women in hats carrying a basket between them on the beach, a hill behind them. It is paired with a quote: "They fetch their sea-born treasures home," which is a paraphrase from the poem "Each and All" by Ralph Waldo Emerson: "I fetched my sea-born treasures home."

This photo shows the women on the beach with a basket: seated, standing, lying down with a hill behind them. It is accompanied by a long quote from *The Cup of Youth* by Silas Weir Mitchell, which begins: "How very silent is the sea tonight."

This excerpt is from *The Cup of Youth* by Silas Weir Mitchell (1829–1914). Mitchell was a colorful character with a foot in both the scientific and literary world, not unlike Oliver Wendell Holmes Sr., who was both a physician and a poet. That the women know about this somewhat lesser-known writer (as compared with Byron) is a testament to the breadth of their reading and self-education. The extensive quotation may indicate that the journal was assembled after the trip—the citation and photo are on their own page. Otherwise, someone in the group committed this poem to memory.

Tuesday July 21, 1891

Our lullaby through the night was from the fog horn which continued its melodious measure till after breakfast. The mist cleared gradually, and we had a bright still day to look out on, and a fresh breeze always on the piazza.

The anniversary of the Autocrat's birth is remembered and she finds in the sugar bowl at breakfast some pretty crochetted [*sic*] edging, the handiwork of the Aristocrat, and a small watercolor of the pier promised.

While at table William came in with mail, bread, etc., said he was all night coming from Boston in the fog.

After the morning work we pitched into the weekly wash, three at the tub, and one on the ice chest reading aloud. When the clothes were spread on the grass we hastened to the piazza and finished Kenilworth.

Lunch served on the back piazza after which photographs were taken of the interior, the back of the house, well, etc. Then writing in the vestibule.

The lighthouse keeper of Boston Light, Captain Bates and his little grandson came over in a boat and made us a call as our nearest neighbor, he was quite entertaining for half an hour.

Our letters were ready at five o'clock for the government workmen to mail. After dinner the Aristocrat and Autocrat with much preparation of rubbers, old skirts, pails & spoons, went forth to dig clams for food to-morrow. The Scribe and Acrobat were left to wash dishes, then to meet the other party at the northern end of the isle, to assist in bringing home the clams. With regret they left a ruddy sunset and soon found their friends with light pails, cut hands, long faces, but no clams.

Returning to the piazza, we saw the "pale regent" rise from the water beyond Minot's light, but far from pale, she was as red and large as the sun when last seen. She rose about 8 o'clock and we watched her two hours.

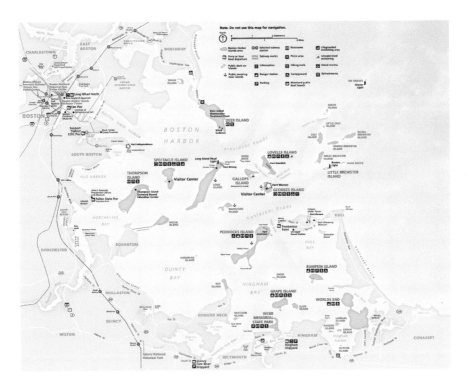

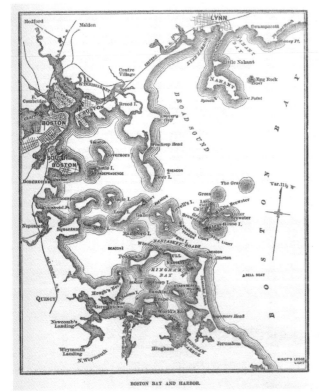

Above: A map of the Boston Harbor Islands National and State Park today. *Courtesy National Park Service.*

Left: "Boston Bay and Harbor" map in the article "The Gateway of Boston" from *Harper's Magazine* European Edition, June–September 1884. *Collection of Suzanne Gall Marsh.*

BOSTON BAY AND HARBOR.

Above: The journal from the first time author Stephanie Schorow examined it at the Schlesinger Library at Radcliffe. *Photo by S. Schorow.*

Left: This vibrant watercolor image from the cover of *Truth* magazine in 1898 presents a fashionable young woman proudly displaying her Kodak. The company's marketing strategy encouraged use of its snapshot cameras to record outdoor activities and scenic views from countryside to seashore. *Courtesy of Martha Cooper Kodak Girl Collection.*

gather clover blossoms for a corsage
to be pressed later — In their wanderings

they interview a man from the number
at work on the wall to ask if he will
take letters to Fort Warren to mail — this
opens a way for sending daily letters
to the city.   Our meals come surprisingly near together dinner tonight consisted of Cold tongue — boiled potatoes.
bread — Orange Marmalade. Cake. Cocoa-
nut Cakes. Maccaroons and Tea — The appetites are all good and everything is
perfectly delicious — After dinner we go
out to the wall to see the work going
on there — The winter storms have thrown

Page 8 of the journal for July 16 includes one of the exquisite watercolors produced during the trip. The initials B.C. indicate this is the work of Bella Coburn. Notice how someone also added a drawing of a four-leaf clover.

up much of the stone work and the men
are replaceing the stones. We sat on the
wall watching the beautiful clouds - the
evening lights in the Light House, and
the steamers proceeding to sea - The Autocrat read aloud from Kenilworth -
altogether it had been a most perfect summer day and night - We sat
late on the piazza with the moon
shining bright and watched the excursion steamers pass - and upon retiring
listen to more from our book in the
dining room - The never failing driftwood gives us ample exercise in fetching it for the kitchen stove -

Page 9 of the journal for July 16 has an illustration of the fuel that the women used for their stove, the driftwood that they gathered on the island.

10

——— Friday. July 17th. ———

This is Acrobatic Verse

In our eastern chamber casement,
Early peeps (or glares) the sun;
And our bird, a meadow lark,
Sings his sweet little song.
Though our beds are rough we sleep well, Morning comes too soon. Every moment is good, night or day.
For breakfast we had
Oat Meal, Hash, Buttered toast, tea and coffee.
"The table was graced with Nasturtiums." the same ones.

The well is still our refrigerator.
William the Swede went to town about eleven. We read Kenilworth on the piazza till lunch

Page 10 of the journal for July 17 includes an impressionistic watercolor of the nasturtiums from "Mr. Dean's garden" that gave the women so much pleasure.

which William brought to us with the mail last night. After dinner instead of our usual walk, we sat on the piazza and enjoyed the beautiful sunset which filled the sky and water with glory, and when the moon, almost at the full, appeared from behind the fleecy clouds we felt that Nature had shown us many of her varying moods on this day. We sat in the moonlight till late conversing as old friends will then betook us to the dining room to read aloud a sermon on Faithfulness, and then a half hour of Kenilworth finished our day.

ye Hot Lobster.

In perhaps the most charming illustration, the artist captures the cooked lobster that the women enjoyed for dinner and includes the image in the entry for July 19.

24.

Our letters were ready at five o'clock for the government workmen to mail. After dinner the Aristocrat and Autocrat with much preparation of rubbers, old skirts, pails & spoons, went forth to dig clams for food to-morrow. The Scribe and Acrobat were left to wash dishes, then to meet the other party at the nothern end of the isle, to assist in bringing home the clams. With regret they left a ruddy sunset and soon found their friends with light pails, cut hands, & long faces, but no clams.

Returning to the piazza, we saw the "pale regent" rise from the water beyond Minots light, but far from pale, she was as red and large as the sun when last seen. She rose about 8 o'clock and we watched her two hours.

Breakfast – Oat meal. Bacon, Fried potatoes
Corn cake, Tea, Coffee.

Lunch – Crackers, Sardines, Cheese, Marmalade,

Dinner – Fried pork & eggs, Baked potatoes, Rice pudding.

This watercolor by Bella Coburn is one of several in the journal painted in the tonalist style, which was prominent in this era. Images of landscapes (and seascapes) were rendered in subtle colors in somewhat abstract and nonnarrative style, meant to evoke emotion rather than represent realistic subject matter. This is page 24 of the journal, July 21 entry.

38.

In the afternoon the weather changed from the sunny dazzling sea, to dark clouds ever varying.

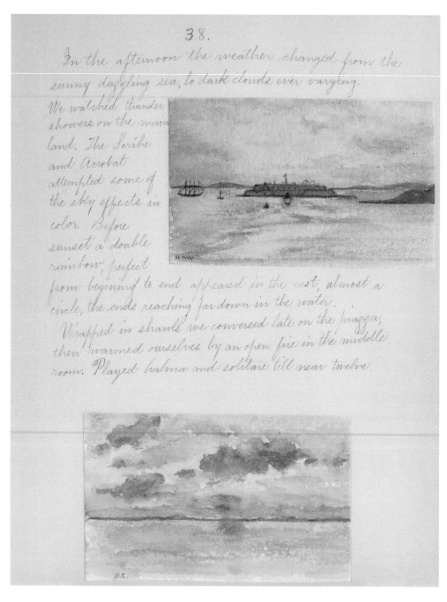

We watched thunder showers on the main land. The Scribe and Acrobat attempted some of the sky effects in color. Before sunset a double rainbow, perfect from beginning to end appeared in the east, almost a circle, the ends reaching far down in the water.

Wrapped in shawls we conversed late on the piazza, then warmed ourselves by an open fire in the middle room. Played halma and solitaire till near twelve.

The illustrations on this page show off the work of both Bella Coburn (*bottom*) and Helen A. Whittier (*top*). They are both in the tonalist style prominent in this time period. Page 38 of the journal, July 25 entry.

Page 42 of the journal for July 26 has an illustration by Bella Coburn of flowers collected on the island. There's a truncated quote from the *King's Handbook* about Great Brewster: "Rich grass and clover cover the bluff, [and columbines] and other dainty flowers thrive."

47

Tuesday July 28th 1891.

Wind S. W. temperature 68°

Breakfast— Oatmeal & Cream.
Hashed tongue—
Corn muffins—
Tea.

Lunch— Crackers & Cheese.
Muffins—
Marmalade— Cookies.
Lemonade—

Dinner— Tomato soup.
Lobster & Dressing
Toast and Tea—
Cold Custard—
Crackers—
Vanilla wafers—

Page 47 of the journal for July 28 integrated the day's menu with illustrations of flowers on the island. The illustrations are so detailed that the flowers can be identified with a smartphone plant identification app. The blue flowers are likely blue chicory, and the yellow flowers are "butter-and-eggs" or toadflax, which bloom during late July.

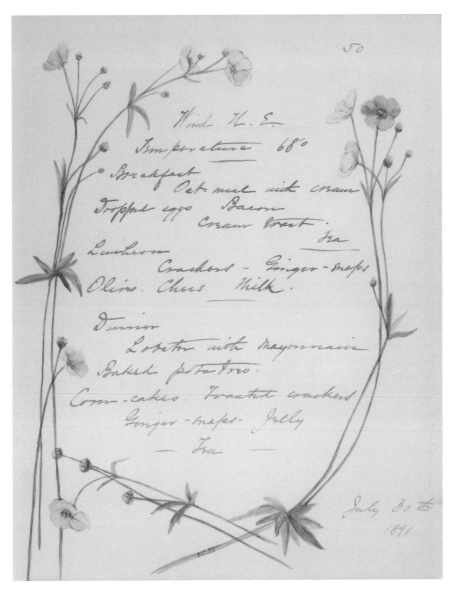

Flowers again grace the day's menu. The initials B.C. (Bella Coburn) are in the stem, but we don't believe the handwriting of this entry is hers, so this is a collaboration. Page 50 of the journal, July 30 entry.

The journal provides us an opportunity to study the geography of the Great Brewster Island in the 1890s; the Boston Harbor Islands constantly change from the forces of wind and sea. This is an excellent view of the east side of Great Brewster showing the sheer cliffs and the erosion. It is also a rare portrait of all four women together. The women seem to have enjoyed walking on the granite wall and talking with the workmen who were rebuilding it. So who took this photo? Could it be one of the men working on the seawall? Notice, too, the large size of the granite blocks used for the wall. This photo appears on page 32 of the journal's July 23 entry.

A more modern look at the seawall on the east side of Great Brewster Island. *Photo by S. Schorow.*

Right: This page from the *Delineator*, a magazine for sewing patterns, shows fashions in the 1890s. Looking at this, it is easy to see why the Merrie Trippers were in what they considered their casual attire on the island.

Below: Seagulls on the seawall observing the mussel beds and sandbar connecting Great Brewster to Little Brewster Island. It is possible to walk between these two islands at dead-low tide, although it is discouraged for safety reasons. *Photo by S. Schorow.*

A more modern view of Great Brewster Island shows the two drumlins and the spit of land that emerges at low tide. Little Brewster and Boston Light are on the right. *Photo by S. Schorow.*

This photo from the journal was taken from the end of the spit of land that emerges at low tide from Great Brewster Island and clearly shows the two drumlins that form Great Brewster Island.

Mills from Rodgers St. Bridge,
Lowell, Mass.

A 1920s postcard of the Whittier Cotton Mill building (*left*) from the Merrimack River built by Moses Whittier in 1878, when Lowell was New England's textile center. In the 1890s, Helen Whittier took over the company after both her father and her brother died. *Courtesy of University of Massachusetts Lowell, Center for Lowell History.*

The brick building that once housed the Whittier Mill can be seen on Stackpole Street in Lowell today. It is now used as public housing, managed by Lowell Housing Authority. *Photo by S. Schorow.*

The final page of the journal is taken up by this watercolor painting by Helen A. Whittier (her initials can be seen) that presents Great Brewster as a mystical island. The quote is from Lord Byron's poem *The Prisoner of Chillon*. The signature at the top right of "Mrs. A.L. Tyler," is from Mrs. Artemas L. Tyler (Florence H. Whittier Tyler, 1862–1936), who was Helen A. Whittier's niece and only surviving relative. She may have owned the journal at one point and added her signature.

23.

— Tuesday July 21. —

Our lullaby through the night was from the fog horn
which continued its melodious measure till after breakfast.
The mist cleared gradually, and we had a bright still
day to look out on, and a fresh breeze always on the piazza.
The anniversary of the Autocrat's birth is remembered
and she finds in the sugar bowl at breakfast some
pretty crochetted edging, the handiwork of the Autocrat,
and a small water color of the pier promised.

While at table William came in with mail, bread &c
said he was all night coming from Boston in the fog.

After the morning work we pitched into the weekly
wash, three at the tub, and one on the ice chest reading
aloud. When the clothes were spread on the grass we
hastened to the piazza and finished Kenilworth.

Lunch served on the back piazza after which photographs
were taken of the interior, the back of the house, well &c.
Then writing in the vestibule.

The lighthouse keeper of Boston light Captain Bates
and his little grandson came over in a boat and
made us a call as our nearest neighbor, he was quite
entertaining for half an hour.

This is page 23 of the journal and the first page of the entry for Tuesday, July 21. To see
page 24, which continues this entry, see the color section.

Breakfast – Oatmeal, Bacon, Fried potatoes, Corn cake, Tea, Coffee
Lunch – Crackers, Sardines, Cheese, Marmalade
Dinner – Fried pork & eggs, Baked potatoes, Rice pudding

NOTES ON JULY 21

This entry was vital to our efforts to identify the Trippers. "The anniversary of the Autocrat's birth" is celebrated, and the day of July 21 matches the birthday of Helen Frances Ray French, who would have turned forty-eight years old. She and the other women were well into middle age when they undertook this Great Brewster adventure, more evidence of the women's spirit and spunk. Note the kind of gifts: crochet and promised watercolor, likely by the Artistic Acrobat, Bella Coburn.

While three of the women do the wash, which is spread on the grass, a fourth reads—which seems like a jolly way to get work done. Again, this may show how the trip was meant to demonstrate "cooperative housekeeping." Recall that two of the women (Helen Whittier and Bella Coburn) were not married, and neither would get married. The fact that all four were dear friends is remarkable.

There is reference to writing in the vestibule. This could include working on the journal but also the letters that they would give to the men working on the seawall to post. Did the women also keep personal diaries? Note that they are now relying on the government workers to deliver their mail.

Something common in the nineteenth century were the social amenities that come from calling on neighbors. During the day, the women received a caller or guest—their "neighbor," in this case, the lighthouse keeper of Boston Light, Captain Thomas Bates. Captain Bates served as Boston Light lighthouse keeper from July 1864 to April 1893.

Bates came by boat, likely because he was with his grandson, but it was and still is possible—if difficult—to walk from Little Brewster to Great Brewster. As noted in the first chapter, sheep used to cross over from Little Brewster to Great Brewster, until the unfortunate day they were caught in a storm and drowned.

The writing in this entry is particularly well crafted. In perhaps the wittiest entry, the writer—who may be Bella Coburn—describes a failed effort to bring home clams for dinner by the Aristocrat and the Autocrat, who return chagrined and empty-handed. Putting that failure behind them, the women

This photo in the journal accompanies the entry for Saturday, July 18, and is captioned "Ye Lunch al fresco." Lunch is served "contrary to preceding custom at the round table in the vestibule." Note the white tablecloth from "Mrs. Partridge" and the wilting nasturtiums from Mr. Dean's garden that grace the Merrie Trippers' table one last time.

watch a reddish moon rise from the water beyond another lighthouse, Minots Light. Officially named Minots Ledge Light, this is a lighthouse about a mile offshore from the South Shore communities of Cohasset and Scituate.

The women watched the moon rise for two hours—the kind of calming experience that any of us who have been on vacation and had the luxury of time could relate to. They refer to the "pale regent," a frequent metaphor for the moon, found in various bits of literature of the day.

The entry ends with a watercolor of Boston Light and the moon, one of the best illustrations in the journal. It was done by Bella Coburn, who adds her initials. Almost as an afterthought, the writer adds the three hearty meals of the day. Coburn seems to be incorporating tonalist style, which was prominent in the art of this era. Images of landscapes (and seascapes) were rendered in subtle colors in somewhat abstract and nonnarrative style, meant to evoke emotion rather than represent realistic subject matter. See this page in the color section.

This illustration from an issue of the *Delineator* magazine (an issue that also featured a story on Helen A. Whittier) shows how the waist remained the focal point of the women's fashion silhouette through the nineteenth century. While the Merrie Trippers did wear hats and long skirts on the island, they were definitely in casual wear.

Also of note: photographs that seem to be taken on July 21 appear in the journal with the entries for July 15 and 16.

Wearing the proper clothing for the occasion was part of the nineteenth-century woman's daily life. The journal describes the women changing into different clothing to begin their trip and then, on their return, changing back to the clothes that apparently were characteristic of their place in society. As one writer said of the Autocrat, she "[shed] her Brewster Chrysalis and [appeared] as a gay butterfly of fashion." Another journal entry records a change to "old skirts" for clam digging.

Two of the images in the 1891 journal in particular show the kind of clothing worn by Ye Merrie Trippers: the pen-and-ink illustration used in the front of this book and the dreamy photo of "Ye Aristocrat Contemplateth Ye Fort." Photos of the women show how each sported a different kind of hat. These images allow us to examine the often elaborate—if not excessive—detail and design in place throughout the 1800s, as well as a preview to the looser, more relaxed styles to arrive and evolve in the twentieth century.

We see our Merrie Trippers wearing summer dresses with high necklines, noticeable collars, fitted long sleeves puffed out on the shoulder and skirt lengths touching the ankle. The movement suggests lightweight fabrics, such as cotton, gauze and linen, which could easily have been woven in a Lowell or other local textile mill. Gone are cumbersome layers of petticoats and enormous, underlying wire hoops and cages that ensured fullness of the skirt.

While the shape of the dress was simpler, more elegant and easier to wear and undergarments lighter or fewer, the waist remained part (if not the focal point) of the women's fashion silhouette through the nineteenth century, including the 1890s. Well-to-do American women typically felt they had to be "in style," and they were influenced by European designers.

Initially, French designers (starting with the Louis XIV era) set the "mode" by sending a special client a wooden doll with movable limbs dressed in the newest costume design for her to wear and be seen in.

Illustrations and photographs of the latest in-fashion creations were soon put to paper, published and sold in fashion magazines. Many women would ask their seamstress or dressmaker to reproduce a costume for them. Dressmakers, who usually worked independently in one of the few "respectable" women's jobs, were very highly skilled. They could transform a "fashion plate" (hand-colored engraving or lithograph) found in women's magazines such as the *Delineator* or *Godey's Book* into a stunning three-dimensional form: conceptualizing a whole outfit comprising numerous odd shapes for the "pattern" and selecting fabrics that they would cut and sew together, like a puzzle, and in the correct measurements for right size and good fit.

This "paper puzzle" for the more privileged set evolved with the invention of what was to become the dress pattern for general usage by the mid-1850s. Ebenezer Butterick, together with his wife, Ellen Augusta Pollard Butterick, invented tissue paper patterns in multiple sizes. In 1863, the couple began selling them out of their home in Sterling, Massachusetts, and the product revolutionized home sewing, according to the *Delineator*, a monthly publication from the Butterick Corporation in New York City, which promoted itself as "A Journal of Culture, Fashion and Fine Arts." Butterick was an inventor and fashion businessman, and the *Delineator* was created as a major vehicle to market patterns of its publisher (Butterick) rather than as a source of fashion advice. Four major pattern companies—Butterick, along with Vogue, McCall's and Simplicity—soon produced patterns of lightweight paper for use in the home, and the pattern industry evolved into a mass fashion supplier.

Today, pattern companies have largely merged or dwindled, while smaller new companies fill special niches, using largely online methods. While Isaac Singer may be credited with the 1851 patented invention of the sewing machine, numerous persons before and after him developed and/or patented new stitches and parts that together created a machine sturdy enough for frequent use, according to Mary Bellis in *History of the Sewing Machine*.

As factories began mass-producing clothing with the aid of sewing machines, large department stores arrived on the scene and provided women with additional, easy to obtain options for their clothing and fashion needs. When the Jordan Marsh department store opened on Washington Street in Boston, the *Boston Post* referred to it as "the most colossal store the world ever saw." The business remained in operation in the "Downtown Crossing" area for more than 150 years. William Filene's and Sons Co. (known to many generations of Bostonians simply as Filene's) opened across the street in 1881, operating for more than a century in Boston. In 1912, it was housed in a still-striking flagship building by Daniel H. Burnham, which is the Chicago architect's only design in Boston. Filene's, however, is long gone.

Thus, by the 1890s, women like our Merrie Trippers had a variety of sources at their disposal for everyday and special outfits—able to "be in fashion" and express their individual sense of style.

WEDNESDAY, JULY 22, 1891

[Page is labeled 24½]
"Every sunrise in New England is more full of wonder than the pyramids, every sunset more magnificent than the Transfiguration. Why go to see the Bay of Naples when you have not yet seen Boston Harbor?" James Freeman Clarke

Wind south east—temperature 1 P.M. 68°
Breakfast   Oat-meal   Dry Toast   Scrambled Eggs   Bacon   Tea   Coffee
Luncheon
Crackers   sardines
Cold Rice pudding   Marmalade   Cocoa
Dinner   Cold fish with cream   Boiled potatoes   Stewed tomatoes
Tea   Cakes

Scribe and Aristocrat prepared the breakfast as the sister had an extra sleep, spending the entire night in the one bed for the first time. The morning work soon disposed of so that at 10 we began *Henry Esmond*. It was a breezy morning after a foggy early one and quite cool. The Scribe put letters upon some linen pillow-cases the Aristocrat is now embroidering for her [sister?]. The Acrobat made some lovely sketches for the glorification of this book. The men are about their lobsters, a buyer coming for them in a boat, a dingy little craft with patched sails. We have a new man here who came Saturday last with William who came from town that day. This man looks a stolid honest creature, tanned by much exposure. The man who left on Sat. was unique. As he came out in the dorry [dory] to meet us. As we went to the mooring Wed. last, he reminded me immediately of Rogue Riderhood. He

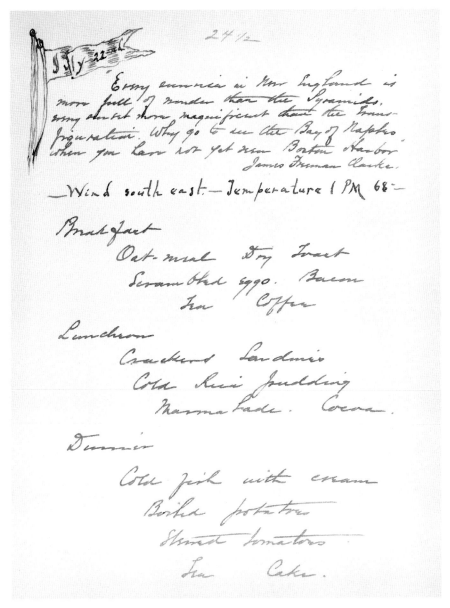

This page was numbered 24½ of the journal and is the first page of the entry for July 22. An otherwise dull recitation of the day's menu is enhanced by a sketch of a banner on a flagpole announcing the day and a snippet of poetry romanticizing beautiful Boston Harbor. We did not include an image of page 25 in this book.

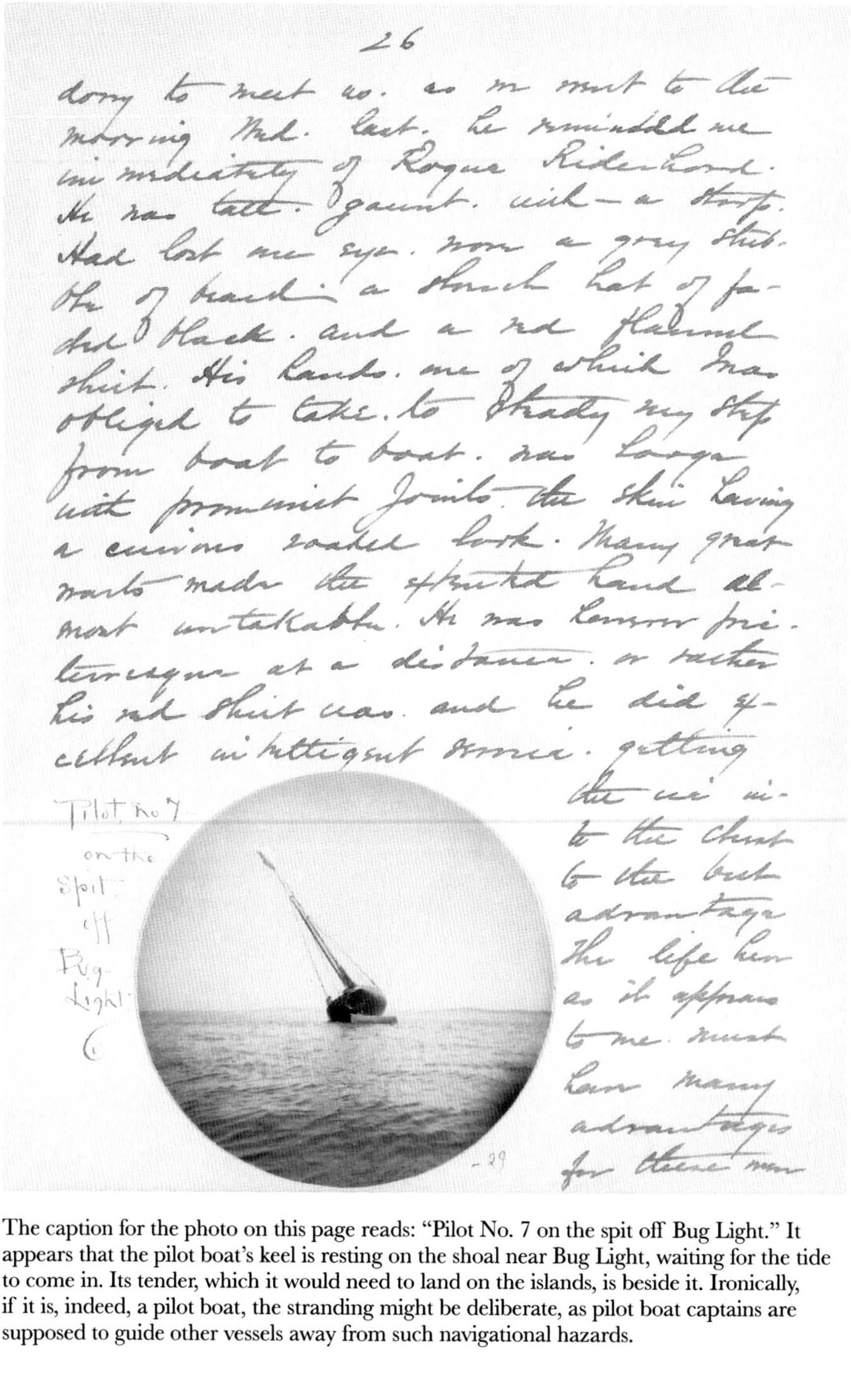

26

dory to meet us. as we went to the mooring shed last. he reminded me immediately of Rogue Riderhood. He was tall. gaunt. with a stoop. Had lost one eye. wore a grey stubble of beard. a slouch hat of faded black. and a red flannel shirt. His hands. one of which I was obliged to take. to steady my step from boat to boat. was large with prominent joints. the skin having a curious soaked look. Many great warts made the afflicted hand almost untakable. He was however picturesque at a distance. or rather his red shirt was. and he did excellent intelligent service. getting the [illegible] to the [illegible] to the best advantage. The life here as it appears to me. must have many advantages for these men

The caption for the photo on this page reads: "Pilot No. 7 on the spit off Bug Light." It appears that the pilot boat's keel is resting on the shoal near Bug Light, waiting for the tide to come in. Its tender, which it would need to land on the islands, is beside it. Ironically, if it is, indeed, a pilot boat, the stranding might be deliberate, as pilot boat captains are supposed to guide other vessels away from such navigational hazards.

27

They are perhaps always of the sailor
class. and if not here. would be either
at sea. doing all the hard service
there required. or living about one
mis ports. in crowded ill-smelling
places. Here is all the free sweet
space. abundant good water. all
the wood one requires. and to them
who can manage a boat. and all
these men can. easy access to towns
So it seems an enviable sort of a lot
to fall to these men. King's Handbook is my authority for saying
this island covers thirty five acres.
Across the "curving gravelly ridge stands
Bug-light. 1½ miles away this light
built in 1856 stands on heavy iron sup-

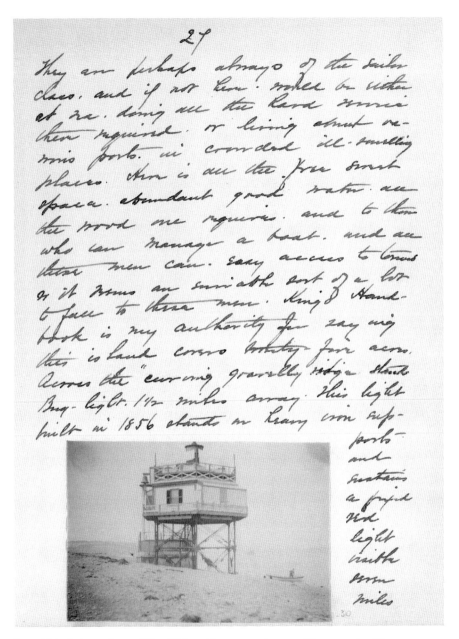

ports-
and
sustains
a fixed
red
light
with
seven
miles

Page 27 includes a photo of Bug Light with someone in a small boat nearby. The photographer was fascinated by this structure.

was tall, gaunt, with a stoop. Had lost one eye, wore a grey stubble of beard, a [indecipherable] hat of faded black and a red flannel shirt. His hands, one of which I was obliged to take to steady my step from boat to boat, was larger with prominent joints, the skin having a curious [indecipherable] look. Many great warts made the extended hand almost untak[e]able. He was [indecipherable] picturesque at a distance, or rather his red shirt was, and he did excellent in [indecipherable] getting the ice into the chest to the best advantage. The life here, as it appears to me, must have many advantages for these men.

They are perhaps always of the sailor class, and if not here, would be either at sea doing all the hard [indecipherable] there required, or living about various ports in crowded ill-smelling places. Here is all the free great spaces, abundant good water, all the wood one requires, and to them who can manage a boat, and all these men can, easy access to towns so it seems an enviable sort of a lot to fall to these men. *King's Handbook* is my authority for saying this island covers twenty-five acres. Across the curving gravelly ridge stands Bug-light, 1-½ miles away. This light built in 1856 stands on heavy iron supports and sustains a fixed red light visible seven miles.

Boston Light is a trifle over eight miles from Boston and 1-⅓ from Point Allerton across main ship channel. As early as 1679 there was some kind of a beacon on the Great Brewster. A light-house built in 1716 was repaired in 1757 after a fire and stood till 1776 when it was blown up by the retreating British marines, it having been held by them three months after the evacuation of Boston. The present structure was erected in 1783 and is 98 feet above sea level. We had a most perfect and glorious night which we spent upon the piazza till the moon arose then in the dining-room when after Halma, there was more of *Henry Esmond* then to bed at 11.10.

NOTES ON JULY 22

The date of this entry is contained in a drawing of a pennant. The entry begins with a quote from James Freeman Clarke (1810–1888), an author, abolitionist and theologian who advocated for human rights, including women's suffrage. The women may have known of his work, or they might have taken the quotation from the title page of *King's Handbook*, where it was reproduced. New Englanders, especially Bostonians of this era, were not reticent about proclaiming the wonders of their homeland. However,

28

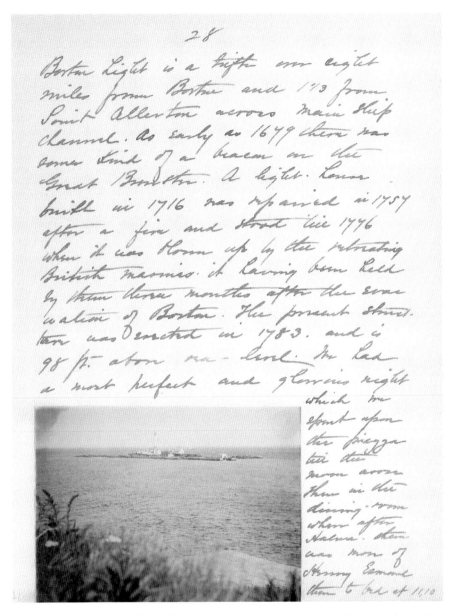

Boston Light is a trifle over eight
miles from Boston and 1½ from
Point Allerton across main ship
channel. As early as 1679 there was
some kind of a beacon on the
Great Brewster. A light house
built in 1716 was repaired in 1757
after a fire and stood till 1776
when it was blown up by the retreating
British marines it having been held
by them three months after the evacuation of Boston. The present structure was erected in 1783. and is
98 ft. above sea-level. We had
a most perfect and glorious night
which we
spent upon
the piazza
till the
moon arose
then in the
dining-room
where after
Halma. there
was more of
Henry Esmond
than to tell of 1510

Page 28 contains a view of Little Brewster Island showing the pier, the lighthouse keeper's house and the assistant keeper's duplex. Boston Light is very faint in the photograph.

the context of this quote from Clarke's book *Every-day Religion* indicates he is talking about the wonders of nature that can be seen in everyday life. He precedes the quote cited this way: "Every little brook which creeps through the meadow is full of wonders of life. Every cloud that drifts past, has lights and shadows more tender than any artist can copy." This can be seen to mirror the women's experience as they delight in the sights and sounds of the island and relish the domestic tasks.

One of the highlights of this journal is its descriptions and photos of harbor landmarks such as Bug Light. A popular subject for postcards in the 1900s, this structure cut a distinctive silhouette in its perch on the long spit that stretched from Great Brewster. At high tide, it seemed to float on the water; at low tide, it could be visited with a walk from Great Brewster. More formally known as "The Narrows Light," Bug Light was constructed in 1856. Harrison Loring was the builder of the lighthouse, and most people who saw it thought it resembled a bug—hence the nickname. The structure was thirty-five feet above sea level, and its light could be seen seven nautical miles away. Over the years, there were many rumors and stories of Bug Light and the many keepers who managed it. One of the most popular stories was of the keeper, James Turner, who was rumored to be both a pirate and a murderer, and it was said that he buried treasures on the harbor islands. On June 7, 1929, Bug Light burned down. The lighthouse keeper

Bug Light. Boston Harbor, Mass.

Bug Light was a popular subject for postcards in the early twentieth century, as this image from a card collected by Stephanie Schorow shows.

was doing some external repairs on the structure when it caught on fire and was destroyed. It was replaced by a gas-operated, lighted bell buoy in 1930. Bug Light has gone through several incarnations. The current Bug Light is a lighted, small, steel tower in the same location as its predecessors.

The History of Henry Esmond is a historical novel with a rather saucy theme by William Makepeace Thackeray, originally published in 1852. Thackeray's other classic novels include *Vanity Fair* and *The Luck of Barry Lyndon*.

One striking aspect of this entry is the vivid description of the sailor accompanying William, who reminds the writer of Roger "Rogue" Riderhood, a character in Charles Dickens's novel *Our Mutual Friend*. To her, his rough appearance speaks of the difficult, at times ugly, life this man may have lived. Even though the trip to Great Brewster brought the women into close company with people who make their lives by the sea (fisherfolk, lighthouse keepers, seawall masons), in this man she observes something that moves her to ponder his life. Whether her speculations are correct, she is compassionate in her musings. She is grateful for the labor he provides in filling the ice chest and appears somewhat relieved by the idea that the old sailor might now be able to lead a restful and fulfilling life among the islands of Boston Harbor.

THURSDAY JULY 23, 1891

Mislabeled as Friday, July 24

Temperature 66° – Wind N.E.
Breakfast – by Autocrat & Acrobat
Oatmeal – Coffee – tea –
Breakfast Bacon – Fried potatoes
Dry Toast – Pop-Overs
Lunch
Crackers – Olives – Quince Preserve
Cake – Orange Marmalade – Lemonade
Dinner –
Cold Tongue Baked Macaroni with Tomatoes
Baked potatoes – Custard Pudding – Tea

Our melancholy friend the Foghorn sounded through our morning dreams, but when we roused ourselves and gazed from our chamber window into

"The ever silent spaces of the East,
Far-folded mists, and gleaming halls of morn."

We found that the sun was triumphing over the fog—and the day proved to be most gloriously clear and beautiful. The sky was almost cloudless and the sea most

"Deeply, darkly—beautifully blue."

From the piazza we could not only see the Gilded Dome shining like a planet on the horizon but could also distinguish the spires of Trinity, the Old South, and Brattle Street Churches, while the afternoon sun brought out with equal distinctness the Nantasket Shore. We have waited for just such a day to climb the cliff back of the house which is the highest land in Boston Harbor and commands a beautiful view. Accordingly all but the Autocrat walked up the hill just before lunch.

The cool refreshing breeze made

"The tides of grass break into foam of flowers
And the wind's feet shine along the sea."

With the aid of the glass, we could see Lovell Island, Marblehead Neck, Egg Rock - Nahant and all the intervening points, while at our feet lay Calf Island and Green Island, homes of humble fisher-folk, and our sister islands the Middle and Outer Brewsters. The Middle Brewster is owned by Mr. Augustus Russ and Mr. Whitney of Boston who have built commodious Summer homes on its rocky ledges and their steam launches, the *Galatea* and the *Iris*, ply to and fro almost daily. The Outer Brewster, the most picturesque of all, is inhabited by four fishermen's families who live in rough shanties. The Island is owned by Mr. Benj. Dean, who intended at one time to build a summer residence upon it, but there being no safe anchorage near, he gave up the plan and leased the Great Brewster instead, upon which we are now domiciled.

The Great Brewster lacks the grandeur and picturesqueness of the other Brewsters having no rock nor ledges upon it and like Deer Island, Long Island, Port Allerton and other lands in the Harbor, has been sadly eaten away by the waves of centuries; the Great Sea Wall which stops these ravages supplies the place of craggy rocks in our evening strolls, and the convenience of good well-water and abundant driftwood go far to compensate in our eyes

29

Friday July 24

Temperature 66° — Wind N.E.

Breakfast —— by Autocrat & Acrobat —
Oatmeal - Coffee - Tea ——
Breakfast Bacon - fried potatoes,
Fry Toast - Pop-Overs

Lunch ——
Crackers - Olives - Quince Preserve
Cake - Orange Marmalade -
Lemonade

Dinner ——
Cold Tongue - Baked Macaroni with Tomatoes.
Baked potatoes —
Custard Pudding - Tea.

Our melancholy friend the Foghorn
sounded through our morning dreams, but
when we roused ourselves and gazed from
our chamber window into
"The ever silent spaces of the East,
Far-folded mists, and gleaming halls
of morn."

Page 29 of the journal. This page is labeled Friday, July 24, but is more likely the first page
of the entry for Thursday, July 23. The next journal entry is also labeled Friday, July 24,
and there is no entry that is labeled Thursday, July 23. Also, the menus (and weather) are
different for each day. At the bottom of the page is a line from the poem "Tithonus" by
Alfred Lord Tennyson.

— 30 —

we found that the sun was triumphing over the fog — and the day proved to be most gloriously clear and beautiful. The sky was almost cloudless and the sea most.

"Deeply, darkly, beautifully blue."

From the piazza we could not only see the Gilded dome shining like a planet on the horizon, but could also distinguish the spires of Trinity, the Old South, and Brattle St. Churches, while the afternoon Sun brought out with equal distinctness the Nantasket shore. The have waited for just such a day to climb the cliff back of the house which is the highest land in Boston Harbor and commands a beautiful view. Accordingly all but the Autocrat

This is page 30 of the journal and the second page of the entry for Thursday, July 23. The line of poetry is from Lord Byron's *Don Juan*. The accompanying photo gives an excellent overall view of the island showing the cottage and several other buildings as well as two of the women. One of the women carries an umbrella. Given the description of a clear, sunny day, perhaps she carries it as protection from the sun.

31

walked up the hill just before lunch.
The cool refreshing breeze made

"The tides of grass break into foam of flowers,
And the wind's feet shine along the sea."

With the aid of the glass we could see
Swell Island, Marblehead Neck - Egg Rock -
Nahant and all the intervening points, while
at our feet lay Calf
Island and Green Island,
homes of humble fisher-
folk, and our sister
islands the Middle
and Outer Brewsters. The Middle Brewster is
owned by Mr. Augustus Russ and Mr. Whitney
of Boston, who have built commodious summer
homes on its rocky ledges and their steam
launches, the Galatea and the Iris ply

Page 31 of the journal and the third page of the entry for Thursday, July 23. The brief quote is an adaptation of a line from the poem "Laus Veneris" by Algernon Charles Swinburne. The two photos on this page show the views that the women enjoyed upon reaching the top of the cliff.

for the absence of more romantic qualities. Turning to descend the steep bluff we see before us our own beloved Brewster stretching out a friendly arm towards the Narrows to bear aloft a torch for the incoming ships when night envelopes all in darkness. We see our dear old house, scene of so many revels, and looking across Nantasket Roads we see Hotel Pemberton and Hull with its more elegant habitations and we descend to our lunch with the "contented mind" which "is a continual feast."

The afternoon and evening were spent upon the piazza, excepting one or two forays for firewood for the sake of exercise, and while one read from *Henry Esmond*, the others watched the majestic ships which with all sails set, flew before the wind. After this gloriously fine day, the sun set in a gray cloud which boded no good for the morrow and for the first time in several days we had a commonplace sunset. It is always an interesting moment, however, for at the appointed time the light flashes from the Light House the flag falls from Fort Warren, and the sunset gun booms. Music from the Excursion boats in the Harbor, was wafted to us, and we could see the lighted trains of cars crawling to and from the Pemberton around Point Allerton and when the friendly lights gleamed all along the horizon from Crescent Beach to Minot's Light, we could not feel that we were far from the Hub of the Universe. At last we adjourned to the dining room for Halma and Solitaire but were delighted to have a call from Mr. Wardrupp who brought us letters, papers and what is fully as important, Roast Beef, Bread and Tomatoes. He left immediately to continue his moonlight sail with a party of friends and after reading our letters we "turned in" about eleven o'clock.

NOTES ON JULY *23*

This entry is labeled July 24, but we believe it is actually for July 23. Perhaps for the writer, like many of us on vacation, the days seem to blend together. The writer more than makes up for the error by penning an exceptionally illuminating entry, with numerous citations of poetry and some actual explanations of the history of the islands. The pages of this entry feature landscape photos, so this may be the most documentary-like of all the entries.

The reference, "ever silent spaces of the East," is from the poem "Tithonus" by Alfred Lord Tennyson, about a man who asks for immortality but neglects to ask for eternal youth and finds himself aging but unable to die. Its most famous couplet is "Man comes and tills the earth and lies beneath / And after many a summer dies the swan." Such romantic melancholy was popular in Victorian era arts.

The line "Deeply, darkly—beautifully blue" is from *Don Juan*, the famous narrative poem by Lord Byron, who seems to be quite a favorite among the Trippers. Here is the full verse:

> *O! "darkly, deeply, beautifully blue,"*
> *As some one somewhere sings about the sky,*
> *And I, ye learned ladies, say of you;*
> *They say your stockings are so (Heaven knows why,*
> *I have examined few pair of that hue);*
> *Blue as the garters which serenely lie*
> *Round the Patrician left-legs, which adorn*
> *The festal midnight, and the levee morn.*

Notice that the citation is slightly off, which might imply this—like other quotes—came from memory.

The views on this day were particularly spectacular. The women could see the Gilded Dome, a reference to the gold-topped Massachusetts State House, which was designed by Charles Bulfinch and built in 1798. Trinity is a reference to Trinity Church, the soaring structure in Copley Square designed by Henry Hobson Richardson and finished in 1872. (The previous Trinity Church on Summer Street was destroyed in the Great Boston Fire of 1872). The rector of the church from 1869 to 1891 was the influential theologian Reverend Phillips Brooks. The Old South is a reference to the Old South Meeting House, one of the most historical churches in Boston. Such a sight is not possible today, as so many high rises have been built along Boston's shoreline and the shoreline itself has been extended significantly with landfill.

On such a lovely day, three of the women decide to make the trek to the north drumlin to enjoy the views. One of them brought a camera and created some spectacular photos that capture the sweep of Great Brewster Island. The record of their trek includes the citation:

> *"The tides of grass break into foam of flowers*
> *And the wind's feet shine along the sea."*

32

to and fro almost daily. The Outer Brewster the
most picturesque of all, is inhabited by four
fishermen's families who live in rough shanties.
The Island is owned by Mr. Benj. Dean, who
intended at one time to build a summer residence
upon it, but there being no safe anchorage near,
he gave up the plan and leased the Great
Brewster instead, upon which we are now domiciled.
The Great Brewster lacks the grandeur
and picturesque-
ness of the
other Brewsters,
having no
rocks nor
ledges upon it
and like
Deer Island,
Snag Island
Point Allerton
and other
lands in the
Harbor, has been sadly eaten away by the
waves by centuries; the great Sea Wall which
stops these ravages supplies the place of
craggy rocks in our morning strolls, and

Page 32 of the journal. This is the fourth page of the entry for Thursday, July 23. The photo captures what the text describes: with no rocks to absorb the impact of the waves against the shore, considerable erosion of the island has taken place. Four women with their sun hats lounge atop the wall. Who took this picture? For a photo of the same area in 2010, see the color midsection.

This is from the poem "Laus Veneris," by Algernon Charles Swinburne. Here is the complete and correct verse:

Ah yet would God this flesh of mine might be
Where air might wash and long leaves cover me,
Where tides of grass break into foam of flowers,
Or where the wind's feet shine along the sea.

The writer's version is slightly off—again, does this mean that it was written from memory?

The entry references Mr. Augustus Russ and Mr. Whitney of Boston, who were members of the Boston Yacht Club.

Another poignant sentence again references Oliver Wendell Holmes's characterization of Boston (in particular its State House) as the "Hub of the Solar System."

It is always an interesting moment, however, for at the appointed time the light flashes from the Light House [Boston Light] the flag falls from Fort Warren, and the sunset gun booms. Music from the Excursion boats in the Harbor, was wafted to us, and we could see the lighted trains of cars crawling to and from the Pemberton around Point Allerton and when the friendly lights gleamed all along the horizon from Crescent Beach to Minot's Light, we could not feel that we were far from the Hub of the Universe.

Note that metaphorical inflation has already set in; Boston is now the Hub of the Universe (not just the solar system), which is, indeed, how most Bostonians today remember that quote.

Like watching television together, reading was a group activity for the Merrie Trippers. On this day, some watch the sunset while one reads aloud from William Makepeace Thackeray's novel *Henry Esmond*. Their games of Halma and Solitaire are interrupted—with delight—by a visit from Mr. Wardrupp, who interrupts a night sail to bring the women letters and paper (perhaps newspapers?) and, as they put it, most importantly, food. Wardrupp is with a party of friends, so it's clear he's not a mere fisherman but of the same social class of the women—or else he would not have letters for them.

Those who have camped on the Boston Harbor Islands would certainly have enjoyed this kind of meal delivery service; the women's descriptions underscore the experience of staying overnight there—that sense of being both near to and far from Boston. The delighted women read their letters and turn in at 11:00 p.m.

The "sunset guns" refers to the military practice of firing a cannon at sunset every night. This practice continues today on the USS *Constitution,* which is docked in the former Charlestown Navy Yard, now part of Boston National Historical Park.

Friday July 24, 1891

Wind SE — temperature 68°
Breakfast –
Oatmeal
Bacon-fried mush and potatoes
Toast and coffee –
Lunch –
Crackers and cheese
Marmalade and Cakes
Dinner –
Roast beef and potatoes
Stewed tomatoes
[undecipherable] and cake

"1765 July 24[th.] Went a-frolicking on the water"
Diary of Col. Samuel Pierce, Dorchester.

Not so this day in '91. It is our first rainy day, and the sea is all muffled in gray.

The day is spent in the commodore's room with work and reading. The rain comes in showers and the stone masons go to the little cow house for shelter.

The Acrobat carries our letters to them as they depart and they kindly take them to mail – Toward night the clouds break and we have the loveliest sunset of all with a double rainbow in the East – Later the mist gathers again and the horn at Boston Light blows through the night - and a steamer answers in the darkness – So damp is everything that we have an open fire – and spend the evening playing Halma and Solitaire.

35

Friday July 24th 1891.

Wind S.E. — Temperature 68°.

Breakfast — Oatmeal.

Bacon — Fried mush and potatoes

Toast and coffee —

Lunch.

Crackers and cheese —

Marmalade and Cakes —

Dinner — Roast beef and potatoes —

Stewed tomatoes —

Cocoa and cake —.

"1765. July 24th Wen[t] a frolicking on the water"

Diary of Col. Saml Pierce,

Dorchester.

Not so this day in '91 — It is one great rainy day and the sea is all muffled in gray

Page 35 of the journal and first page of the entry for Friday, July 24.

NOTES ON JULY 24

Once again, the Trippers rely on *King's Handbook of Boston Harbor*. The quote from Colonel Samuel Pierce appears on the handbook's title page. Samuel Pierce Jr. (1739–1815) was, according to Historic New England, a farmer who became a supporter of the American Revolution. He kept a record of his experiences and wrote acute observations of the patriotic effort. The Pierce family papers are in the collection of Historic New England, which also maintains the Pierce House in Dorchester. It's unclear if the Trippers were familiar with Pierce's writing, but one of the women apparently recognized the date of July 24 from *King's Handbook*. Alas, July 24, 1891, was not a day for frolicking in the sea, as it was gray and damp.

This is a short entry by the writer who tends to use dashes instead of periods. There's a reference to "the little cow house," which might be the shelter for the Lady Brewster, the cow that lives on the island. The journal contains a charming photo of the bovine. The women very much rely on the stonemasons working on the seawall to deliver their letters.

Two photos are matched together on a page in this section. One shows "Ye Aristocrat and Ye Acrobat" as they "go a-wading." Do they actually swim in the water? It would be warm enough in July. The other photo does not identify the women but contains this verse:

> *The maidens lean them over*
> *The water the waters, side by side*
> *Mrs. Browning.*

The quote is from the first two lines of the third stanza of Elizabeth Barrett Browning's "A Romance of the Ganges" which was first printed in Finden's *Tableaux* in 1838.

SATURDAY, JULY 25, 1891

Breakfast – Oatmeal, Fried mush, Fried potatoes, Warmed beef, Tea, Coffee. – Lunch – Raw tomatoes, Cold tongue, Crackers, Cheese, Marmalade, Milk. – Dinner – Roast beef, Boiled potatoes, Stewed tomatoes, Cake, Tea. –

36.

The day is spent in the Commodore's room with work and reading — The rain comes in showers and the stone masons go to the little cow house for shelter. The Acrobat carries our letters to them as they depart and they kindly take them to Neal — Toward night the clouds break and we have the loveliest sunset of all with a double rainbow in the East. Later the mist gathers again — and the horn at Boston Light blows through the night — and a steamer answers in the darkness — So damp is everything that we have an open fire — and spend the evening playing Halma and Solitaire.

Page 36 of the journal and the second page of the entry for Friday, July 24. The photo is a nicely centered shot of the house showing the large piazza on which the women enjoyed quiet activities. Note the well in which the women stored their food while waiting for a delivery of ice for the ice chest.

Yᵉ Aristocrat and yᵉ Acrobat
go a-wading ⟶

"The maidens lean them over
the waters, side by side."
mrs. Browning.

Top photo is labeled "Ye Aristocrat and ye Acrobat go a-wading." Note that they are not swimming. The quote for the bottom photo, "The maidens lean them over the waters, side by side," is from the poem "A Romance of the Ganges" by Elizabeth Barrett Browning.

37

Saturday, July 25th. 1891.

Breakfast — Oat meal, Fried mush,
Fried potatoes, Warmed beef, Tea, Coffee —

Lunch — Raw tomatoes, Cold tongue, Crackers,
Cheese, Marmalade, Milk. —

Dinner — Roast beef, Boiled potatoes,
Stewed tomatoes, Cake, Tea. —

Morning, warm bright
and still. Many are the
beautiful pictures in sky
and sea, in ships and
neighboring shores.

We read and sewed on
the piazza till high
noon, when the Acrobat
and Aristocrat, "Like little wanton boys, who swim
on bladders all day long, yet scarce beyond their
depth," went in wading. The water was cold, but
great fun. As we came from lunch to the
piazza we found we were just too late to see the
incoming and outgoing Cunarders pass each other.
Finished Henry Esmond.

Page 37 of the journal is the first page of the entry for Saturday, July 25. The photo accompanying the day's account is of sailboats of various types slowly plying the calm waters of the harbor in the "warm, bright, and still" morning. Their skippers await the gentle puff of wind that will fill their sails and send them on their way. To see page 38, go to the color section.

Morning warm, bright and still. Many are the beautiful pictures in sky and sea, in ships and neighboring shores. We read and sewed on the piazza until high noon when the Acrobat and Aristocrat, "Like little wanton boys who swim on bladders all day long, yet scarce beyond their depth," went in wading. The water was cold, but great fun. As we came from lunch to the piazza, we found we were just too late to see the incoming and outgoing Cunarders pass each other.

Finished *Henry Esmond*.

In the afternoon the weather changed from the sunny dazzling sea, to dark clouds ever varying. We watched thunder showers on the mainland. The Scribe and Acrobat attempted some of the sky effects in color. Before sunset a double rainbow, perfect from beginning to end appeared in the east, almost a circle, the ends reaching far down in the water.

Wrapped in shawls we conversed late on the piazza, then warmed ourselves by an open fire in the middle room. Played halma and solitaire till near twelve.

NOTES ON JULY 25

"Many are the beautiful pictures" might be an allusion to "I have the sky and ocean framed before me like a beautiful picture" in Charles Dickens's *Out of Town*. The "Like little wanton boys..." quote is adapted from Shakespeare's *King Henry VIII*, Act 3. "Cunarders" probably refers to passenger ships operated by the Cunard Line, sailing in and out of Boston.

The entry also notes that the "Scribe and Acrobat attempted some of the sky effects in color." You can see their results in the color section.

The women were ever mindful of their appearance even while swimming. Indeed, swimming is linked with the action of "little wanton boys." Throughout the 1800s, modesty drove bathing attire for women. In the first half of the century, women had to remain completely covered and could not expose skin. They wore to the beach what was referred to as a bathing gown. This was a long dress from shoulder to knees. They then wore trousers underneath plus stockings. The material was usually made of wool, flannel or cotton. When wet, the material would get very heavy. Some of these bathing gowns also had weights sewn in so that when the gown got wet it wouldn't float up. Clearly this prevented women from swimming or other water activities.

Later in the 1800s, the Princess Suit was introduced, a one-piece suit consisting of a long-sleeved blouse cinched at the waist into long pants. In addition to the suit, women would wear a skirt to hide their shapes. Again, it was not practical and would weigh women down in the water. However, the Princess Suit did evolve, and by the late 1890s the pants had shortened under the skirt and the sleeves started to become shorter. The Princess Suit was the beginning of what would become the one-piece bathing suit.

Sunday, July 26, 1891

Wind S.W.
Temperature 72°
Breakfast –
Oatmeal and cream
Potatoes with cream
Scrambled eggs corn-cakes, tea coffee

Dinner
Warmed up roast beef
Baked potatoes – Broiled tomatoes
Ginger-snaps – crackers – cheese

Tea
Sardines – dry toast
Cakes – chocolate

A warm still morning. Many small craft sailing about. Others at anchor, those on board fishing. Some of them drop anchor here at our mooring and parties of men, mostly very young and very active, explore the island from [the] bluff. The "Posy" comes in at two just as we are about sitting down to our dinner. Mr. Wardrup apologizes for neglecting to bring the mail and offers to take us for a sail to Hull or elsewhere, which is declined. Aristocrat and Acrobat have a wade in the high water alongside the ruined pier. We read Irving's most charming papers found in the Sketch Book, "Westminster Abbey" and "Stratford upon Avon", also some articles in a [indecipherable] Christian Register. "Some Reason For Becoming A Catholic" and "From Roman Catholicism to Unitarianism" and the edition [indecipherable].

39

Sunday July 26th, 1891
Wind S. W.
Temperature 72°
Breakfast —
  Oat-meal and cream
    Potatoes with cream
Scrambled eggs. Corn-cakes
      Tea Coffee

Dinner — Warmed-up roast beef
Baked potatoes — Broiled tomatoes
  Ginger-snaps — Crackers — Cheese

Tea
  Sardines — dry toast —
  Cake — Chocolate.

The first page of the July 26 entry starts off, as usual, with the menu. The entry ends on page 42 with an illustration of wildflowers in a jar. This page is in the color section.

Our early after-noon dinner gave us time for a long sunset walk following the wall its entire length, then the beach. The sunset was very beautiful. Very soft and and [*sic*] tender colors in the [indecipherable] clouds. The evening was still, very still. The lights along shore casting long [indecipherable] reflections in the calm water.

NOTES ON JULY 26

This entry is written in the same thick, nearly indecipherable hand that had penned the earlier entries for July 18 and July 22 and the later entry for July 30. The interval of four days between each entry with such a distinctive penmanship clearly indicates that the Merrie Trippers took turns chronicling their adventure. Unlike earlier records by this writer, there is no cartoon-like sketch to highlight the date of the entry. Instead, the narrative is accompanied by a photograph of a boat at anchor while sailboats and steamers ply the harbor in the background. A painting by Bella Coburn of a glass jar containing daisies, clover, grasses and other flowers decorates the journal entry. Under the painting is a description from *King's Handbook of Boston Harbor* of wildflowers on Great Brewster: "Rich grass and clover cover the bluff and other dainty flowers thrive."

The menu for the day hints at a change in schedule for the second Sunday of the women's sojourn. Lunch is omitted in favor of dinner at two o'clock in the afternoon followed by tea later in the day—the only time that afternoon tea is mentioned in the journal.

The day begins peacefully, but it is not long before the quiet of the "warm still morning" is broken by groups of "very young and very active" men who have come to energetically explore the island. Even today, weekend activity on the Boston Harbor Islands increases noticeably and dramatically over that of weekdays, as visitors, free from work and other obligations, arrive to enjoy the special spaces in their own ways.

Just as the women settle down to dinner, the *Posy* arrives, bringing "Mr. Wardrup"—another spelling of the name of this man—but no mail from the mainland. As noted in the Hull Yacht Club's *Handbook* for 1891, the *Posy* was one of the cutters or sloops enrolled in the Hull Yacht Club and was owned by Russell G. Hunt of Weymouth. The women apparently decline an offer of a sail to Hull, and the Aristocrat and the Acrobat go wading, as they had the day before. The Merrie Trippers spend the rest of their afternoon on literary and intellectual pursuits.

The women enjoy two essays by Washington Irving (1783–1859), an American writer who spent a great deal of time in Europe, mostly in England. His *Sketchbook* is a collection of short stories that includes "Westminster Abbey" and "Stratford-on-Avon," as well as the better-known "Rip van Winkle" and "The Legend of Sleepy Hollow." "Westminster Abbey" is Irving's somber account of a wander through the tombs, memorials and monuments of England's Westminster Abbey while he reflects on life, death and the transient nature of memorials and the lives they are designed to immortalize. On that Sunday afternoon in 1891, the women would have read: "Time is ever silently turning over his pages; we are too much engrossed by the story of the present, to think of the characters and anecdotes that gave interest to the past; and each age is a volume thrown aside to be speedily forgotten." How amazed would these late nineteenth-century women have been to learn that early twenty-first-century readers of their journal would take such interest in their "characters and anecdotes."

Irving's essay "Stratford-on-Avon" is a narrative of his self-described "poetical pilgrimage" to William Shakespeare's hometown and place of burial. Perhaps the Merrie Trippers, lovers of literature that they were, dreamed of their own literary pilgrimage someday.

The women then turned their attention to more contemporary concerns and perused several articles in the *Christian Register*, a weekly newspaper published by the American Unitarian Association in Boston. According to americanunitarian.org, the publication carried religious and secular news, including the doings at the Massachusetts State House, Congress and local courts, as well as book reviews and religious poetry. We were unable to locate a copy of the edition the women read, but the August 22, 1891 edition of the *Sacred Heart Review*, a Catholic publication, contained a scathing rebuttal of the essay "From Roman Catholicism to Unitarianism," characterizing it as the "very weak article" that had been published in "our esteemed contemporary." The timely rebuttal in a newspaper published a month after the women's vacation indicates that the issue of the *Christian Register* the women read was not one that had been left behind in the house by last season's tenant, but one that they themselves had brought with them or that had been timely delivered to them during their stay. Recall that Helen Augusta Whittier was active in Unitarian organizations, having participated in the incorporation of the Channing Fraternity in 1884 as noted earlier in this book. No casual beach reads for these women!

Because the women had eaten dinner earlier that afternoon and could be satisfied with a light repast at the end of the day, they had time to enjoy a long walk while admiring the changing colors among the clouds as sunset approached shortly after 7:00 p.m. With other visitors now returned home, the Merrie Trippers have the island nearly to themselves again, and the day ends as it began—in stillness.

MONDAY, JULY 27, 1891

Thermometer 66° wind—W.N.W.
Breakfast
Minced tongue and potato
Buttered toast
Oatmeal – tea

Lunch
Crackers – cheese – olives
Gingersnaps – milk

Dinncr
Beef stew
Tomato sauce
Cake – chocolate

> *"and there on breezy morns*
> *They saw*
> *The fishing schooners*
> *Outward run,*
> *Their low-bent sails*
> *In tack*
> *And flaw*
> *Turned white or dark*
> *To shade and sun"*

The morning dawned calm and clear with not a ripple on the sea.

> *"At dawn the fleet stretched miles away.*
> *On ocean plains asleep, –*
> *Trim vessel waiting for the day*

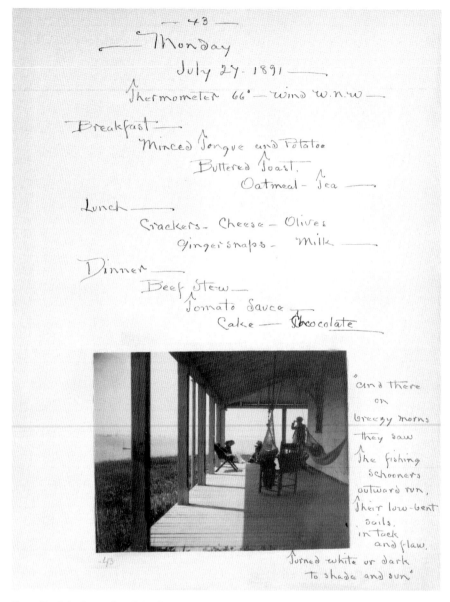

— 43 —
— Monday
July 27·1891 —
Thermometer 66° — Wind W.N.W —

Breakfast —
Minced Tongue and Potatoe
Buttered Toast.
Oatmeal — Tea —

Lunch —
Crackers — Cheese — Olives
Ginger snaps — Milk —

Dinner —
Beef Stew —
Tomato Sauce —
Cake — Chocolate

And there
on
breezy morns
they saw
The fishing
Schooners
outward run,
Their low-bent
Sails,
in tack
and flaw,
Turned white or dark
To shade and sun"

Page 43 of the journal and the first page of the entry for Monday, July 27. A few lines from John Greenleaf Whittier's poem "The Tent on the Beach" follow the weather report and the day's menu. In the photo, the four women lounge on the sunny piazza. One looks out to sea, while another rests in the hammock. We are left to wonder, "Who took the picture?"

To move across the deep.
So still the sails they seemed to be
White lilies growing in the sea."

But about 10 a.m. we observed a vivid streak of blue water beyond Lovell's Island showing that a breeze had sprung up and in a short space of time, the expanse of water on either side of us had changed its whole appearance and color, from the pearly gray placidity which reflected every object however distant to the intense rippling blue, while every sail far and near sprang from listlessness into sudden activity. As has happened nearly every day, the wind freshened as the hours wore on and in the afternoon, the Square Partie were fain to quit the breezy piazza and seek the seclusion which the fence could grant. There basking in the sun, we continued the reading of "A Social Departure" by Sara Jeannette Duncan, a very amusing book which we had begun before lunch.

Our Knights of Labor who are repairing the Sea Wall did not appear today and have not worked since last Friday when the rain drove them home, so our mail communication with the outer world seems more precarious than usual. This did not prevent the writing of some letters to be dispatched at the first opportunity. William went to Boston this morning and returned in the evening with our ice, which was very welcome though the Well is an admirable refrigerator.

After dinner we gathered gaily about the crackling wood fire and gossipped [*sic*] for a half hour then adjourned to the Commodore's Room for a game of Euchre, in which either luck or skill seemed to remain on one side, which side shall not here be revealed. Later while reading aloud we received a batch of letters from William and also a box of delicious candy sent by a faithful XV. This made a cheerful ending to an uneventful but delightful day.

NOTES ON JULY 27

The quote beginning "And there on breezy morns" is from the poem "The Tent on the Beach," from *The Works of John Greenleaf Whittier*, also published as a separate piece in 1867. Appropriately, the poem "The Tent on the Beach" recounts a story of three young men who, in about 1867, did an excursion much like what the Merric Trippers did in 1891, pitching

— 44 —

The morning dawned calm and clear,
with not a ripple on the sea.
  "At dawn the fleet stretched miles away,
    On ocean plains asleep,—
  Trim vessels waiting for the day
    To move across the deep.
  So still the sails they seemed to be
    White lilies growing in the sea."

  But about 10 a.m. we observed a
vivid streak of blue water beyond Swell's
Island showing that a breeze had sprung up,
and in a short space of time the expanse
of water on either side of us had changed
its whole appearance and color, from the
pearly gray placidity which reflected every
object however distant, to the intense rippling
blue, while every sail far and near sprang
from listlessness into sudden activity. As has
happened nearly every day, the wind freshened
as the hours wore on, and in the afternoon
the Square Parties were fain to quit the
breezy piazza and seek the seclusion
which the fence could grant. There basking

Page 44 of the journal and the second page of the entry for Monday, July 27. The poetry quoted here is from "Morning and Evening by the Sea" by James Thomas Fields (1817–1881).

a tent on the beach, as did some other campers in the same area. The poem describes what they did, the people they encountered and their meditations on the place and their experiences. The women must have appreciated the parallels to their own Great Brewster adventure. John Greenleaf Whittier was a famed abolitionist, novelist and poet. Greenleaf Whittier was born in 1807 in Haverhill, Massachusetts. His family were Quakers, and he had no formal education—nor did the family have a lot of money. He began writing and was passionately antislavery. He worked early on in menial jobs while he began writing poetry. He then worked in Boston for several abolitionist newspapers and magazines. He became editor of the *New England Weekly*. He began to get involved in politics and in 1831 ran unsuccessfully for Congress. In 1842, he formed the Anti Slavery Party and by the 1850s worked on the formation of the Republican Party. From 1844 to 1846, Whittier edited an antislavery newspaper, the *Middlesex Standard*, which was published in Lowell. He published many works; his most famous was *Snow-Bound*. He was good friends with Lucy Larcom who had been a Lowell mill-girl for ten years and whose poetry he published in an abolitionist newspaper. Whittier submitted Lucy Larcom's first book to his own publisher for eventual publication. (See July 29 entry for a sample of her poetry.)

The second poem quoted is from "Morning and Evening by the Sea," by James Thomas Fields (1817–1881), a poet, editor and publisher. He was also a partner of William Ticknor in the Old Corner Bookstore and later served as an editor of *The Atlantic* magazine. Fields is another example of a prominent Bostonian who had contact with many of the literary lights of the day.

Note the women now return to reading *A Social Departure* by Sara Jeannette Duncan, which they describe as "very amusing."

Despite the distance from Boston, the women seem to be very much in communication with the mainland through the efforts of the faithful William, who also brought them ice. Someone in the XV Club even sent a box of candy. There's no mention of money exchanging hands, but we can't help but wonder if William was paid for his efforts. Did he live alone and enjoy interacting with the women? He certainly helped make their stay on the islands much more pleasant. See the July 27 entry in the journal in the color section.

45

in the sun, we continued the reading of "A Social Departure" by Sara Jeanette Duncan, a very amusing book which we had begun before lunch.

Our Knights of Labor who are repairing the Sea Wall did not appear today and have not worked since last Friday when the rain drove them home, so our mail communication with the outer world seems more precarious than usual. This did not prevent the writing of some letters to be despatched at the first opportunity. William went to Boston this morning and returned in the evening with our ice, which was very welcome though the Well is an admirable refrigerator.

-44

Page 45 of the journal continues the journal entry for Monday, July 27. The photo depicts one of the Merrie Trippers having a not so merry time fetching their food from the well that served as "an admirable refrigerator" when no ice was available for the ice chest.

46

After dinner we gathered gaily about the crackling wood fire and gossipped for a half hour - then adjourned to the Commodore's Room for a game of Euchre, in which either luck or skill seemed to remain on one side, which side shall not here be revealed. Later while reading aloud - we received a batch of letters from William and also a box of delicious candy sent by a faithful XV. This made a cheerful ending to an uneventful but delightful day.

The Lady Brewster

Page 46 is highlighted by a portrait of "The Lady Brewster," who is apparently a cow that lived on the island. We don't know if Her Ladyship provided the milk that the women drank. We certainly hope she did not go near the freshly laundered clothes the women had placed on the grass to dry in the sun. Page 47 of the July 27 entry can be found in the color section.

TUESDAY, JULY 28, 1891

Wind S.W. Temperature 66°
Breakfast—Oatmeal and Cream
   Hashed tongue
   Corn muffins
    Tea

Lunch Crackers and cheese
Muffins
Marmalade—Cookies
Lemonade
Dinner tomatoe [*sic*] soup
Lobster and Dressing
Toast and tea
Cold custard
Crackers
Vanilla wafers

A lovely morning—The Scribe and the Aristocrat go to Bug Light for pictures. A gentle breeze brings the clouds together so it is not so clear as when they started. A schooner and tug going through the channel add to the views. They gather stones for a dish of lilies for the winter. There is a sprinkle of rain to hurry them home.

The afternoon is spent in reading "A Social Departure" and the evening with work. Halma and Cards in the dining room.

NOTES ON JULY 28

A pleasant description of a "typical day" on the island: observing the weather, enjoying meals, taking in the views, outdoor activities, then indoors for reading and games in the evening.

The illustrations on the first page of the entry (see this in the color section) are Bella's floral watercolors of blue chicory and "butter-and-eggs" or toadflax, a yellow flower that blooms during late July. Even though a few of the pictures correspond to the activity in the entry, any of them may have been placed for aesthetics rather than accuracy by date. For example,

48.

A lonely morning. The Scribe and Austocrat go to Bug Light for pictures — A gentle breeze brings the clouds together so it is not so clear as when they started — A schooner and tug going through the channel add to the views — They gather stones for a dish of lillies for the muter — There is a sprinkle of rain to hurry them home — The afternoon is spent in reading "A Social Departure" and the Evening with work Halma and Cards in the dining room —

The second page of the July 28 entry (see the first page of July 28 in the color section) features three photos, probably not all taken on that day. There are three figures near Bug Light in the top photo but only two mentioned in the entry. One photo has all but faded.

137

This evocative photo was taken at the end of the spit that forms from Great Brewster Island and reaches toward Georges Island and Fort Warren. Hence the journal's caption reads, "Ye Aristocrat Contemplateth Ye Fort."

the Bug Light photo with three women doesn't quite match the entry, which says there were two who went to Bug Light. Close examination of the beach stones, in "Ye Aristocrat Contemplateth Ye Fort," shown above, and "Fort and Narrows" on July 27 (page 25), indicates they were taken at the same time. This kind of non-synchronous placement occurs throughout the journal.

The photo of the Aristocrat, Elizabeth Dean, at the end of the land spit from Great Brewster looking at Fort Warren on Georges Island, recalls the words of John Stilgoe, the Harvard professor who found the journal, in his book *Alongshore*:

> *And caught in tide, in wind, in the glare of reflected and refracted light, standing against wavy vastness, the woman stands as more than experienced observer. She becomes something else, a vertical element on the beach, an object of view, a seamark, a landmark.*

WEDNESDAY, JULY 29, 1891

Breakfast—Oatmeal. Baked Potatoes. Sally Lund. Fried Lobster
Lunch—Sardines. Crackers. Custard. Ginger Snaps
Dinner—Salt fish. Broiled Potatoes. Macaroni with tomatoes,
Cake. Tea

> *"The vessels are sunk in the mist*
> *And hist!*
> *Through the veil of the air*
> *Throbs a sound*
> *Like a wail of despair*
> *That dies into stillness profound.*
> *All muffled in gray is the sea,*
> *Not a tree*
> *Sees its neighbor beside*
> *Or before:*
> *And across the blank tide,*
> *Hark! That sob of an echo once more."*

Warm gray fog. A quiet uneventful day. Some of the rooms were prepared
for the guests who come after us.
The usual reading, writing and work.
Our parlor fire was lighted early in the afternoon.

NOTES ON JULY 29

The poem after the day's menu are the first two stanzas of "The Fog-Bell"
by Lucy Larcom (1824–1893), which refers to Harding's Ledge, off Point
Allerton in Hull, marked by a large, sonorous bell buoy. According to *King's
Handbook*, "The mournful peal of the bell breaks through the gray solitudes
with that strange pathetic harmony which Lucy Larcom has thus described."
The poem concludes:

> *'Tis the fog-bell's imploring, wild knell!*
> *It is well*
> *For the sailors who hear;*

49.

Wednesday, July 29th,

Breakfast — Oatmeal. Baked potatoes. Sally Lunn. Fried lobster.
Lunch — Sardines. Crackers. Custard. Ginger snaps.
Dinner — Salt fish. Boiled potatoes. Macaroni with tomatoes
Cake. Tea.

"The vessels are sunk in the mist   All muffled in gray is the sea;
        And hist!   Not a tree
Through the veil of the air   Sees its neighbor beside
        Throbs a sound   Or before;
Like a wail of despair   And across the blank tide,
That dies into stillness profound. Hark! that sob of an echo once more."

Warm gray fog. A quiet uneventful day. Some of
the rooms were prepared for the guests who come after us.
The usual reading, writing and work.
Our parlor fire was lighted early in the afternoon.

This entry, the first page for July 29, includes a watercolor mirroring the fog of Lucy Larcom's poem "The Fog-Bell," cited here.

But its toll
Thrills the night with a fear; –
To what doom drifts the rudderless soul !

The women could likely hear that bell and had either memorized or added Larcom's poem.

Lucy Larcom worked in the Lowell mills from age eleven to twenty-one. She was a friend of John Greenleaf Whittier. It's interesting that Lucy Larcom, a mill girl from Lowell, should apparently have spent some time in Hull, a popular vacation spot for all classes, before the Merrie Trippers stopped there. She heard the bell buoy at Harding's Ledge and was so moved by its melancholy sound that she wrote this poem.

The single page of the entry includes an unsigned watercolor that captures how the women were experiencing the fog. It seems to perfectly match Larcom's poem.

Sally Lund cake is still popular today.

THURSDAY, JULY 30, 1891

Wind N.E.
Temperature 68°
Breakfast
Oatmeal with cream
Dropped eggs bacon
Cream toast tea

Luncheon
Crackers   ginger snaps
Olives Cheese   Milk

Dinner
Lobster with mayonnaise
Baked potatoes
Corn-cakes Toasted crackers
Ginger-snaps   Jelly
tea

51

This morning rain and cloudy. Unusual bustle of house-work. Sweeping and dusting. preparing for the new-comers who are expected on Sat. next. The square party will go to Hull tomorrow. weather permitting. and from there to Boston and home. Had letters in the afternoon. the young men from Federal St. running down in their yacht to bring them. There was much walking on the spit and beach for pebbles. and for gathering of wood. as the supply was low. Late in the afternoon clouds thickened. and still later fog settled down. to the ? that of making the horn a necessity. but later yet. that too cleared away. and the outlook is more promising for the morrow.

This is page 51 of the journal and the second page of the July 30 entry. Page 50 can be found in the color section.

The morning warm and cloudy. Unusual bustle of house-work, sweeping and dusting, preparing for the newcomers who are expected on Sat. next.

The "square partie" will go to Hull tomorrow, weather permitting, and from there to Boston and home. Had letters in the afternoon: the young men from Federal St. running down in their yacht to bring them. There was much walking on the spit and beach for pebbles and for gathering of wood as the supply was low. Later in the afternoon, clouds thickened, and still later fog settled down to the extent of making the horn a necessity, but later yet that fog cleared away and the outlook is more promising for the morrow.

NOTES ON JULY 30

The women are contemplating the end of their stay. They have an eye to the next day's weather, and they dutifully clean house for the house's next guests, which indicates that they are not the only party to stay on the island that summer. Throughout the trip, they handle the daily chores methodically and without complaint. Once they are home and the adventure is over, it seems likely that these are the sorts of duties that will be done for them by their servants.

The first page of this entry is embellished with a watercolor by Bella Coburn of yellow buttercup-like flowers. It is difficult to determine if this image was painted on the island and the text added later. See this page in the color section.

FRIDAY, JULY 31, 1891

We were awakened on this, the last morning of our stay, by the melancholy note of the Fog-Horn, which has come to have a friendly, protecting sound to us. The Autocrat and Aristocrat prepared our last breakfast while the others made the last attempts at "slicking up" the house, although the state of the atmosphere without, seemed to preclude the possibility of our leaving the Island for some time. At last the rain fell in torrents, and we were deciding that we would have another day to finish the "American Girl in London," which we find very amusing, when Frank came up with the news that William was ill and was forbidden by

— Friday July 31 —

We were awakened on this the last morning of our stay, by the melancholy note of the Fog-Horn which has come to have a friendly, protecting sound to us. The Autocrat and Aristocrat prepared our last breakfast while the others made the last attempts at "slicking up" the house, although the state of the atmosphere without, seemed to preclude the possibility of our leaving the Island for some time. At last the rain fell in torrents and we were deciding that we would have another day to finish the "American Girl in London" which we find very amusing, when Frank came up with the news that William was ill - and was forbidden by the Fort Warren Physician to expose himself to dampness. Frank modestly disclaimed the ability to sail us into Hull in such nasty weather, and our only chance seemed to lie in Capt. Bates of the Lighthouse, who might send us over in his boat. But just as we were getting a note ready to send to him, the rain suddenly ceased having washed all the fog away - and to our amazement in ten minutes the Gilded Dome was plainly visible where an impenetrable wall of fog just hung. Shortly it showed such signs of clear weather that William declared it would be dry enough

Unnumbered page in the journal. It is the first page of the Friday, July 31 entry, the final entry.

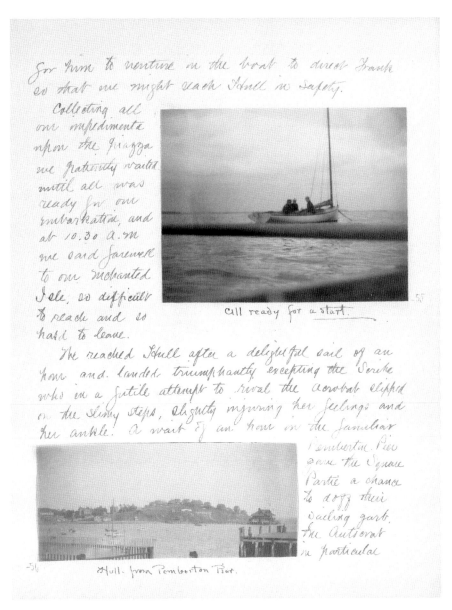

for him to venture in the boat to direct Frank so that one might reach Hull in safety.

Collecting all our impedimenta upon the piazza we patiently waited until all was ready for our embarkation, and at 10.30 a.m we said farewell to our enchanted Isle, so difficult to reach and so hard to leave.

All ready for a start.

We reached Hull after a delightful sail of an hour and landed triumphantly excepting the Scribe who in a futile attempt to rival the acrobat slipped on the slimy steps, slightly injuring her feelings and her ankle. A wait of an hour in the familiar Pemberton Pier gave the Square Partie a chance to doff their sailing garb, the Autocrat in particular

Hull from Pemberton Pier.

Unnumbered page from the Friday July 31 journal entry that has two photos. The top one, captioned "All ready for a start," shows three women in the boat who appear to be waiting for a fourth Merrie Tripper (the photographer) as well as a skipper to unfurl and hoist the sail and get underway. The bottom photo, captioned, "Hull from Pemberton Pier," depicts a scene familiar to the Merrie Trippers, who waited there for hours on the first day of their sojourn and now must wait there another hour on the last day before finally heading home.

the Fort Warren Physician to expose himself to dampness. Frank modestly disclaimed the ability to sail us into Hull in such nasty weather and our only chance seemed to lie in Captain Bates of the Lighthouse, who might send us over in his boat.

But just as we were getting a note ready to send to him, the rain suddenly ceased, having washed all the fog away, and to our amazement in ten minutes the Gilded Dome was plainly visible where an impenetrable wall of fog just hung.

Shortly it showed such signs of clear weather that William declared it would be dry enough for him to venture in the boat to direct Frank so that we might reach Hull in safety.

Collecting all our impedimenta upon the piazza, we patiently waited until all was ready for our embarkation, and at 10:30 a.m. we said farewell to our enchanted Isle, so difficult to reach and so hard to leave.

We reached Hull after a delightful sail of an hour and landed triumphantly, excepting the Scribe who in a futile attempt to rival the Acrobat slipped on the slimy steps, slightly injuring her feelings and her ankle. A wait of an hour on the familiar Pemberton Pier gave the Square Partie a chance to doff their sailing garb, the Autocrat in particular shedding with celerity her Brewster Chrysalis and appearing as a gay butterfly of fashion.

Soon we were speeding towards the Hub in the Nantasket Steamer passing Fort Warren on its unfamiliar side, and looking back regretfully to our Island home. Steaming through the crowd of tempting pleasure yachts, we were in a trice landed at Rowe's [sic] Wharf, whence to our sorrow, our paths diverged. Turning our faces to the work-a-day world, we leave behind us the uneventful idyllic days, like no others in our lives, with their placid serenity, their pleasant spice of labor, the unruffled happiness of accustomed comradeship, and all the glory of sea and sky, now only:

> *"A winter fireside dream*
> *of dawns and sunsets by the Summer Sea."*

Notes on July 31

The "melancholy note of the Fog-Horn," presaged the Merrie Trippers' last day on the island, a tone that had "come to have a friendly, protecting sound" to them. They were saying goodbye not only to a place that had become dear to them, but also to a respite and an adventure, something different from their daily lives at home. The weather, too, seemed reluctant to let them go. They were almost hopeful that the weather would preclude their leaving, but go they must. Despite William the Swede's illness, they were making plans to ask Captain Bates, the lighthouse keeper, for alternative transportation to Hull. Another day's sojourn might have allowed them to finish reading another book by Sara Jeanette Duncan, *An American Girl in London*, a fictional journal of a single woman's solo voyage from New York to England, published in 1891. The women seem to be very taken by the work of Duncan.

Anyone who has ever rented a vacation cottage would be familiar with the routine of transition: "slicking up" the house, gathering their baggage and giving one last, long look at their "enchanted Isle, so difficult to reach and so hard to leave." The photo labeled "Ye Baggage of ye Trippers" shows their bags stacked on the piazza of the cottage, ready for their departure, including a couple of umbrellas that must have come in handy during their stay.

Perhaps this baggage was just their personal belongings, not the entirety of their "impedimenta." In the early pages of the journal, the writer mentions that most of the household goods and groceries had been taken down to Brewster some days before the beginning of their trip. William's recovery coincided with the improved weather, and he and Frank, another island fisherman, safely transported the women to Pemberton Pier in Hull on William's sailboat. The photo labeled "All ready for a start" shows three people in a small catboat, getting ready to shove off. Presumably, they waited for the photographer.

Arriving at Pemberton Pier, the Scribe had a slight incident, slipping on steps as she tried to replicate the Acrobat's more graceful landing. Apparently, her pride was hurt more than her ankle, as no further mention of the accident appears in the journal. The handwriting suggests that the Scribe herself noted this event and did not elaborate on it.

Once in Hull, exchanging their "sailing garb" for their more stylish city clothing completed their metamorphosis, especially for the Autocrat, who apparently took fashion seriously. More significantly, they also shed the identities they had adopted while on the island, identities that allowed them to play different roles and to form their own society, much like people involved in modern role-playing games. The photo labeled "Hull from Pemberton Pier" hints at the distance they were already feeling from their island life.

shedding with celerity her Brewster Chrysalis and appearing as a gay butterfly of Joshim.

Soon we were speeding towards the Hub on the Nantasket Steamer passing Fort Warren on its unfamiliar side, and looking back regretfully to our Island home. Steaming through the crowd of tempting pleasure yachts we were in a trice landed at Rowes Wharf, whence to our sorrow our paths diverged.

Turning our faces to the work-a-day world, we leave behind us the uneventful idyllic days, like no others in our lives, with their placid serenity, their pleasant spice of labor, the unruffled happiness of accustomed comradeship, and all the glory of sea, and sky, now only

"a winter fire side dream
Of dawns and sunsets by the Summer Sea."

This unnumbered penultimate page of the journal for July 31 has two photos without captions: one, rectangular in shape, of Fort Warren in the background; the other, round, showing boats on their moorings. Note how the written text fits around the shape of each picture. This suggests that the text was written after the photos (from two different types of camera) were developed and placed in the book.

This photo from the journal accompanies the Friday July 31 journal entry and is captioned "Ye Baggage of ye Trippers." The Merrie Trippers have packed their belongings in an assortment of suitcases and duffel bags with blankets and various items of outer clothing at the ready and stacked them on the piazza. Note the four furled umbrellas leaning against the post.

On their return trip on the Nantasket Steamer from Hull to Boston's Rowes Wharf, they looked back at Fort Warren, the yachts in the harbor, seen in the photos labeled 57 and 58 in the manuscript, and especially their island home. The fact that one of the photos is in round format and one is rectangular indicates that they were taken with two different cameras, perhaps by two different people aboard the Nantasket Steamer. Once they reached Boston, "the Hub," they resolutely turned their faces to the work-a-day world, leaving behind "the uneventful, idyllic days like no others" in their lives, with their "placid serenity, their pleasant spice of labor, and the unruffled happiness of accustomed comradeship, and all the glory of sea and sky." The labor was light, but for women accustomed to having domestic help, the daily chores and housekeeping were perhaps a novelty that gave some structure to their days. In typical New England fashion, activities like gathering wood and foraging for clams, albeit unsuccessfully, allowed them to have fun exploring the island while maintaining a sense of purpose.

The Great Brewster adventure seems to have marked a turning point in the women's lives. Their shared adventure and companionship were a sparkling jewel, and was an experience which perhaps they knew was never to be repeated. When they reached Boston, they all went their separate ways to their individual lives, "whence to our sorrow our paths diverged." What longing is expressed here! They are leaving behind not just a vacation but a lifestyle. "And all the glory of the sea and sky" were now only:

> "A winter fireside dream
> Of dawns and sunsets by the Summer Sea."

This ending quote is from a long poem by John Greenleaf Whittier called "The Tent on the Beach." A haunting ending—the island almost seemed to represent the freedom that the women would lose. We all feel that when we end our vacations, but this seems more poignant. Are they going back to a world where they can no longer be their authentic selves? Or has this unique, shared experience, this special island, given them a new perspective on their everyday lives?

The final illustration is of Great Brewster Island as it appeared at the time of the women's visit, and it is accompanied by a quote from Lord Byron's famous poem *The Prisoner of Chillon* which is about a man imprisoned for years on a remote island who somehow found joy and beauty even from his prison cell. A fuller citation reads: "And then there was a little isle / Which in my very face did smile / The only one in view / A small green isle, it seem'd no more / Scarce broader than my dungeon floor." Byron ends his poem on a poignant note that likely resonated with Helen Whittier: "My very chains and I grew friends / So much a long communion tends / To make us what we are:—even I / Regain'd my freedom with a sigh." See this final page of the journal in the color midsection.

GREAT BREWSTER ISLAND

1900 to 2022

*Since 1979 I have spent countless hours on Great Brewster Island
both in the daytime and evening hours. I believe it is a magical, mystical place
that holds the energies of the former islanders, visitors and various workers
on island-related projects.*
—*Suzanne Gall Marsh, founder of the Friends of the Boston Harbor Islands*

Even if the Merrie Trippers never returned to Great Brewster—as far as can be determined—the island had a colorful history in the twentieth century and into the twenty-first century.

In the late 1800s, the Portuguese fishermen who lived on Long Island were evicted when the City of Boston planned to build an almshouse. Some of these displaced families relocated to Peddocks and the outer islands, including Great Brewster. "From 1900 until 1941, fifteen families leased summer cottages on Great Brewster from the federal government. Among the summer cottagers were colorful characters, such as Frank McKinley, 'Shanghai Harry' Long, Ray Thomas, and Joe 'Peg Leg' Nuskey," according to *The Boston Harbor Islands—An Urban Wilderness* by David Kales.

Families built houses on the island as summer getaways; photographs from the 1930s show perhaps a dozen structures. These families did not own the land, but at a time when there was little oversight by any agencies, people just decided to build there. This means, however, that records of this period are hard to come by. The summer residents coexisted with the fishermen and their families.

Top: A 1937 photograph of Great Brewster shows the diversity and simplicity of the island's structures. *Courtesy of the Massachusetts Department of Conservation and Recreation.*

Bottom: "Five in bathing suits on the beach with dog," 1939. *Courtesy of the Pedersen family grandchildren and siblings Sue and Jim Saint Croix and Sandy Roberts, shared at the 2008 reunion of Great Brewster Islanders.*

In John Lochhead's scrapbook of historic newspaper articles is an August 6, 1938 story, "Hex Haunts Beautiful Brewster Islands," that says,

> *Not that you'd think it was exclusive to look at the dozen odd, flimsy cottages snuggled down in the lee of the westerly bluff. Greater Brewster's exclusiveness is that the United States government owns the island and wants no more summer visitors. Those who owned cottages on it previous to 1917 are allowed to stay upon payment of $5 per year. Just who owns Greater Brewster is something of a mystery, despite the fact the government collects the rent.*

Laura Thibodeau Jones's book *Generations: 1891–1940 Living on the Islands of Boston Harbor* says, "After the devastating Chelsea fire of 1908, my lobster fishing grandfather, August Reekast, took his entire family to Outer Brewster where they lived during the summer months. Finally, after a move to Middle Brewster they settled on Great Brewster, where my mother, Ida Knoll spent much of her youth."

On September 13, 2008, in an effort to record more social history of the island, the Friends of the Boston Harbor Islands sponsored a boat trip and reunion of people who were children in the 1930s and spent summers on the island. Relatives of Great Brewster Islanders also shared photographs and stories. A video recording of the participants' memories was made by the Friends for the Island Voices project.

Nearly all of the people interviewed remember the island being called "Greater Brewster," not Great Brewster. They spoke of their happiness at being on the island and their joy over the freedom to play outdoors all day. They described fathers who had to work "in town" during the week and came out on Friday night with groceries and supplies and returned to Boston on Monday morning.

Francis A. Perry recalled how he and his ten siblings came out to the island in June when school ended and stayed through the summer. They slept four in a bed next to the window where Boston Light flashed its rays. Fishing, clamming and visiting Calf Island were favorite pastimes.

Gerry McVey described having a pet seagull. He told a story of building a boat of orange crates and setting off into the ocean with his younger sister. However, the water began swamping the flimsy craft. His aunt swam out and rescued them.

The Saint Croix siblings, Sue, Jim and Sandy, talked of their grandparents, the Pedersens. Their mother was "the best swimmer on the island," and

"Cottages, cottagers, and boats, September 6, 1939." *Courtesy of the Pedersen family grandchildren and siblings Sue and Jim Saint Croix and Sandy Roberts, shared at the 2008 reunion of Great Brewster Islanders.*

their uncle dated Wanda, one of the Norwood daughters from Boston Light on Little Brewster.

Alas, for the children of Great Brewster, Uncle Sam had other plans. With America's entry into World War II in 1941, the summer cottagers were evicted and the cottages demolished in preparation for the construction of the Great Brewster Military Reservation. "During World War II, a bomb and chemical proof bunker were constructed to serve as a control post for the harbor's underwater minefield in conjunction with control posts on Georges and Deer Islands," according to the *Cultural Landscape Report Boston Harbor Islands National and State Park*, vol. 2 (2017). Both neighboring Calf and Outer Brewster Islands were also developed as military reservations. When World War II ended, the U.S. Army established caretaker status for many of the islands.

Tom Hayden, one of the participants in the 2008 Great Brewster reunion, recalled visiting the island in the 1950s when his uncle was the army caretaker. His aunt and uncle lived in one of the remaining army barracks. There were tunnels and bunkers to explore on the weekend trips with his family.

Eventually, all of the Boston Harbor fortifications were decommissioned and either transferred to the State of Massachusetts or sold at public auction. The May 16, 1953 *Boston Globe* featured a story about the sale, "Great Brewster Island in Harbor Is Sold for $8,150—Paul D. Kiah of Newton Submits Highest Bid at U.S. Auction Here." The story said that Kiah, a U.S. Army and Air Force veteran, was fond of islands. He served on Corregidor, Angel Island in San Francisco Bay, Fort Slocum, New York; and in the Panama Canal Zone. "It's restful looking out on the water," Kiah told the *Globe*. The article also said, "Kiah intends to conduct fishing parties in the Summer. He is an amateur fisherman himself."

In 1972, the Metropolitan Area Planning Council released *The Boston Harbor Islands Comprehensive Plan*, which was prepared for the Department of Natural Resources. Legislation soon followed to establish the Boston Harbor Islands State Park. Great Brewster Island had resident summer island managers for many years. In 1980, Jan Newlin created the Great Brewster Island Self-Guided Tour for park visitors.

The June 26, 1984 *Boston Globe* City Life section featured a story on "The Island Managers," including two women who were among the twenty island managers who lived on the island for the summer. It reports that "the two women watched the city lights in silence from atop a cliff on Great Brewster

The well that served as the Merrie Trippers' refrigerator was used by summer residents on the island in the 1930s and 1940s, as this photo shows. Today, all traces of the well have disappeared. Here we compare images during the 2008 reunion of Great Brewster Islanders. *Photo by S. Schorow.*

Island. The night air over Boston Harbor was clear, and the skyline nine miles distant, glittered across the horizon. Corri Gottesman and Margie Coffin are living in tents, showering with solar heated water and flavoring their meals with wild herbs." One can't help but think of the Merrie Trippers.

Today, if you walk the shores of Great Brewster, you will find no traces of any of the cottages of the 1930s or 1940s or of the cottage where the Merrie Trippers stayed. The well, which served as the refrigerator for the women in 1891 and provided water to the late cottage dwellers, has disappeared. Trails that were once maintained are grown over. You must bushwhack to get to the top of either of the island's mounds, and trees there can block views of the ocean. At low tide, you can walk the spit toward Georges Island, a truly dramatic way to experience the harbor. The Bug Light structure was destroyed by fire in 1929, and as of 2022, a skeletal steel structure topped by a beacon stands in its place. The eighty-nine-foot Boston Light, illustrated by the Trippers, still operates, sending its flashing light every ten seconds, to a range of twenty-seven nautical miles. The seawall remains, if crumbled in spots.

The Friends of the Boston Harbor Islands have sponsored many trips to Great Brewster over the years. These daytime and evening cruises have introduced countless visitors to the wonders of the island. An especially memorable adventure was on October 14, 1989, when the MV *Abigail Adams* ran aground during a Friends trip to Boston Light on Little Brewster. The solution was to walk across the mussel beds to Great Brewster Island, where there was a public pier. The boat company sent a replacement boat, and the 150 visitors saw a rainbow while walking across the mussel beds. Meanwhile, the boat captain and crew had to wait hours for the tide to turn before they were freed to leave.

The Great Brewster pier was severely damaged by storm waves in 1992 and removed by the Massachusetts Department of Environmental Management (DEM). (What was formerly DEM eventually became part of the Massachusetts Department of Conservation and Recreation, which today manages many of the islands in Boston Harbor.) Nearly ten years later, DEM conducted environmental remediation of underground and aboveground storage tanks left from the World War II Great Brewster Military Reservation. Trails were cleared, scenic view spots created and a composting toilet installed. Today, the only access is by private boat.

The "abrasion" or erosion noted in the nineteenth century continues. In 2021, the National Trust for Historic Preservation listed the Boston Harbor Islands as one of the eleven most endangered historic places in

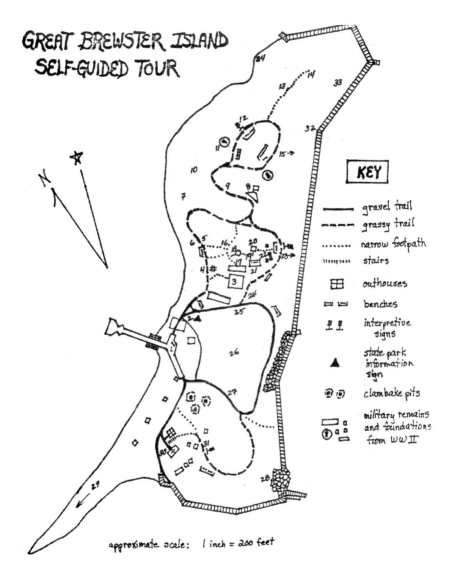

Great Brewster Island self-guided tour map and key created in 1980 by Jan Newlin, the Department of Environmental Management island manager.

America, citing intensifying storm surges and sea-level rise that are due to climate change causing accelerated coastal erosion and escalating loss of archaeological and historic resources. Comparing the photos of the Great Brewster journal to more modern photos gives us a sense of the ever-changing geography of the islands.

Great Brewster has returned to a wild state—perhaps more like it was before the European settlers arrived. It remains a jewel in the islands of the national and state park, a place where visitors can still, like the Merrie Trippers, find it to be "an enchanted Isle, so difficult to reach and so hard to leave."

EPILOGUE

GULL LULLABIES AND FIREFLIES

The impulse to record our adventures seems nearly universal. Nearly one hundred years after the Merrie Trippers' adventure on Great Brewster Island, a member of our team of writers, Marguerite Krupp, spent many days and nights on the Boston Harbor Islands as a volunteer guide. Long before Marguerite had heard of the Merrie Trippers, she, like them, reveled in the sights and sounds of the island and meticulously recorded her impressions and her meals in a journal. Here is an excerpt:

Sunday, June 24, 1990

Friends of the Boston Harbor Islands (FBHI) volunteer Karol Bartlett and I came out on the landing craft from Hingham at 7:00 a.m., which meant getting up around 5:00 a.m. The weather was distinctly unpromising, and the forecast was for thunder showers. We packed to camp, but we agreed if the weather was bad, we'd come back Saturday.

We had signed up as overnight on-island volunteers, and this weekend we were sent to Great Brewster. We explored the island Saturday. Saw and identified a lance-leaf coreopsis and a lovely little blue flax. The flax plant itself would remind you of mustard, with its overlapping, stem-climbing leaves, but the flowers are a lovely shade of blue, darker veined, with a white (mostly) center.

Misty weather greeted the Friends of the Boston Harbor Islands 2011 spring trip to Great Brewster Island. *Photo by Ken Stein.*

Saw some fireflies along the beach. The lights of Boston Harbor wink on and off, too, through the fog. Boston Light's beams just across the water, cast pale rainbows in the mist. The foghorn sounds every few seconds. We can hear the planes overhead a lot tonight—more than during the day. They seem intrusive, while the foghorn just fits.

The gulls "sang" to us all night long—sort of a "gull lullaby." I liked the sound of those two words rolling around on my tongue as if they were one: "Gullullaby." Worthy of Gertrude Stein!

Several gulls are nesting here. Saw some maybe month-old chicks waddling around and testing the water. They're just getting past the fuzz-ball stage. They're gawky, not quite sure of themselves or their role. Their parents are still quite protective. One gull seems to have declared the top of the outhouse as his/her territory. It's funny to hear them land and walk around on top while you're inside. They diligently guard their territory, and they'll dive at you if you come too close. One "christened" one of the volunteers yesterday.

Besides frozen water bottles (for both water and refrigeration), we brought the following food this weekend:

Saturday Lunch: *Water, sandwiches, cookies, oranges.*

Saturday Supper: *Knorr Tomato Basil soup, hamburgers and buns. We also brought "Anasazi Surprise," (a casserole of beans, tomato, cheese, etc.), but it was still frozen at suppertime, so we had it for breakfast. Also had toasted marshmallows and s'mores with the group.*

Sunday Lunch: *Sandwiches again, strawberries and yogurt and Toll House cookies.*
We also picked and ate some early beach peas and gathered some red clover heads for tea,
as well as some artemisia....
We're now waiting for the boat back to Georges, then on to the ferry to Boston. There's a
lot of traffic on the harbor, and the wind's picking up, but most of these small crafts aren't
paying much attention. Can't wait for our next island adventure!

When researching this book, the team was aware that they were looking
into the history of four relatively comfortable, middle-aged white women
who had the luxury of taking two weeks off to go to the Boston Harbor
Islands. What they experienced, however, remains universal to so many
women—the enjoyment of female companionship evidenced by talking into
all hours of the night, taking walks together, reading out loud to each other
and collaborating on meal preparation and cleanup. The team began to feel
like its own band of Merrie Trippers, particularly because most of the team
has spent time on islands in Boston Harbor.

The comparison of this journal to Facebook is apt. The women wanted
to record their experience in some way to share with friends. They were
meticulous but selective. They were able to wash their clothes, keep their food
cool and somehow, somewhere, use a privy. They saw their own surroundings
in the context of the poetry and literature that was so important to their
lives. They have a message for us today—get away from it all and read and
write and walk and think. The journal is a small snapshot of a place in
time—while the four women relaxed on the island for two weeks, the fast-
paced industrial era carried on around them.

Over a span of thirty years, team member Carol Fithian has been a harbor
volunteer, park ranger, boat narrator, FBHI coordinator of volunteers, trainer
and writer. "My nature has always had a compelling sense of adventure,"
she said. "My education and interests have always focused on historical
characters and their relation to place and time. These have had an effect
on most of my choices, in childhood through reading and imagination, and
my career in my adult years. The harbor environment and all of the people
it brought my way wove a tapestry of stories, life portraits and challenges."

The four Merrie Trippers' supportive and creative bond gave them the
reward and the pride of solving the challenges of daily life in an island
atmosphere, Carol says. "Those of us who have camped on the islands feel a
kinship with these women who spent two weeks together."

Team member Vivian Borek felt a connection with the Merrie Trippers
almost immediately due to her own experiences with adventure travel:

"Almost thirty years after my junior year in France, I decided to make new use of my French-speaking skills and love of French culture with solo vacations to Paris and throughout France. Each year up to 2019, I took one, two or three trips to the City of Light and other well-known and hidden destinations. In total, I set foot on nearly 100 different cities and towns throughout France. The four upper-class women who lived in New England more than a century ago probably yearned to experience life devoid of their roles as wives or proper ladies. I, on the other hand, had grown up in a working-class environment, was single, and supported myself. I spoke French, and I wanted to see the world—Europe first because I had learned Romance languages and was of Polish ancestry. People often describe solo travelers as 'courageous' and 'unusual.' Perhaps, like the Merrie Trippers, it's a matter of following a very strong desire to experience more out of your life, void of usual social roles, able to try on a new you, with new people. At the end of my emails I often add an adage that reflects what I've grown to value: 'Accumulate experiences rather than things.'"

Visiting the Boston Harbor Islands still lets visitors connect with the past and discover aspects of themselves. This is true today as much as it was for these four women. The draw of the islands is timeless.

Visiting the Boston Harbor Islands

The Boston Harbor Islands National and State Parks observed two anniversaries in 2022. The state park is fifty years old, and the national park is twenty-five years old. Friends of the Boston Harbor Islands have served the park and its visitors as volunteers since 1979. You can visit the park by seasonal ferry service, or private boat. The peninsulas in the park, which are Deer Island, Nut Island, Worlds End and Webb State Park, can be accessed by ground transportation.

For information on program events and ferry schedules visit:

www.bostonharborislands.org
www.nps.gov/boha
www.thompsonisland.org
www.fbhi.org

DISCUSSION QUESTIONS

1. The four women adopt nicknames and new identities for this journal. Why do you think they did that?

2. Do you see similarities between the ways the women recorded their adventure with camera and journal notes and the way that people today chronicle their vacations with cellphone photos, Instagram and Facebook?

3. There are four different styles of handwriting in the journal. Can you tell them apart? Do you detect differences in personalities among the four women?

4. Were the women, in your perception, "roughing it"? Address the lack of gas lights, the mail delivery, food, the leaky roof and the use of the well as a refrigerator.

5. The four women used quotations from a variety of poetry and literature. Do you see a pattern in these selections? Have you read any of the writers and poets quoted here?

6. Like Facebook, the entries are snippets of a particular moment in time. What details do you find most interesting? What other details would you have liked to see the women include? What details are boring?

7. The women never explicitly speak of women's rights or women's suffrage in this journal. What does that imply—if anything—about their thoughts on this issue? Would you describe these women as "feminists" in the modern sense?

8. The allure of escaping to a deserted or magical island is a theme in many forms of literature and culture. Consider the classics *Robinson Crusoe*, *The Swiss Family Robinson* or *Treasure Island* or even dystopias like that depicted in *Lord of the Flies*. Pop culture references range from the classic *Gilligan's Island* to the film *Cast Away* to the TV series *Lost*. Why are we so intrigued by islands—either magical or dangerous?

9. If you could escape to an island for two weeks, what kind of island would it be?

SOURCES

Sources for this book came from a variety of materials, including books and websites on the Boston Harbor Island; National Park Service websites; genealogical databases, including the U.S. Census; back issues of the *Boston Globe* and other newspapers; the collective knowledge of the Boston Harbor Islands from team members; and Martha Mayo's knowledge of the history of the city of Lowell, Massachusetts. Details on the Helen Augusta Whittier Album can be found at https://www.radcliffe.harvard.edu/schlesinger-library/collections/helen-augusta-whittier-album and Stephanie Schorow, "Roughing It on Great Brewster: Daring Nineteenth Century Women Spend Fortnight on 'Enchanted Isle," *Harvard Gazette*, April 16, 2009.

The history of the Boston Harbor Islands, particularly cited in chapters 4 and 7 and used throughout the notes on the journal entries, is from Moses Foster Sweetser, *King's Handbook of Boston Harbor* (Boston: Moses King Corporation, 1882); Edward Rowe Snow, *Islands of Boston Harbor* (Beverly, MA: Commonwealth Editions, 2002); Christopher Klein, *The Boston Harbor Islands* (Lanham, MD: Globe Pequot Press, 2020); Stephanie Schorow, *East of Boston: Notes from the Harbor Islands* (Charleston, SC: The History Press, 2008); James Henry Stark, *An Illustrated History of Boston Harbor* (Boston: Boston Electrotype Engraving and Manufacturing Company, 1880); *Gleanings from the Records of the Boston Marine Society Through Its First Century 1742–1842*, published by the Society in 1879 and reissued 1999; *Boston Harbor Islands*

Comprehensive Plan (Boston: Metropolitan Area Planning Council, 1972); David Kalcs, *An Urban Wilderness: The Boston Harbor Islands* (Charleston, SC: The History Press, 2007); Pavla Šimková, *Urban Archipelago: An Environmental History of the Boston Harbor Islands* (Amherst: University of Massachusetts Press, 2021); Jeremy D'Entremont, *Boston Light Three Centuries of History 1716–2016* (Portsmouth, NH: Coastlore Media, 2018); Anthony Mitchell Sammarco, *Boston's Harbor Islands* (Charleston, SC: Arcadia Publishing, 1998); Laura Thibodeau Jones, *Generations: 1891–1940 Living on the Islands of Boston Harbor* (Bloomington, IN: Author House, 2011); "The Gateway to Boston," *Harper's Monthly Magazine* (European edition), June–November 1884; *Cultural Landscape Report Boston Harbor Islands National and State Park Volume 2: Existing Conditions* prepared by the Olmsted Center for Historic Preservation, National Park Service, Boston, 2000/2017; Nathaniel Bradstreet Shurtleff, *A Topographical and Historical Description of Boston* (Boston: Boston City Council, 1871); Lucy Larcom, *A New England Girlhood, Outlined from Memory* (Boston: Northeastern University Press, 1986, first published in 1889).

Chapter 1

Background information on the four women and their families from U.S. Census data and Ancestry.com. Information on JB French Sr. from "Contributions of the Old Residents' Historical Association, Lowell, Mass., vol 4," https://libguides.uml.edu/early_lowell/contributions. Details on Artemas Lawrence Tyler (1860–1897) from www.myheritage.com/names/artemas_tyler, and Charles Cowley, *A History of Lowell, Second Revised Edition* (Boston: Lee & Shepard, 1868). We also relied on "Lowell's Oldest Literary Club," *Boston Globe*, March 13, 1893, and "Unique XV Club of Lowell," *Boston Globe*, March 25, 1906; Dean Family Papers, Mss687 R. Stanton Avery Special Collections, New England Historic Genealogical Society, Boston.

Chapter 2

Information on Helen A. Whittier's life came primarily from Mabel Hill, *Helen Augusta Whittier 1846–1925: A Memorial* (Boston: Massachusetts State Federation of Women's Clubs, 1930); Frances Willard, *Occupations for Women:*

A Book of Practical Suggestions for the Material Advancement, the Mental and Physical Development, and the Moral and Spiritual Uplift of Women (New York: Cooper Union, 1897); Helen M. Winslow, "Club Women and Club Life," *Delineator: A Journal of Fashion, Culture and Fine Arts*, October 1899; History Committee of the Federation, *From the Past to the Future: A History of the Massachusetts State Federation of Women's Clubs, 1893–1988* (Canaan, NH: Phoenix Publishing, 1988); Who's Who in America, 1907–1908, plus articles in the *Boston Globe* and the *Lowell Sun*. Also "Panic of 1893," https://www.u-s-history.com/pages/h792.html; Annual Catalog, Lasell Female Seminary, Auburndale, MA, Academic Year 1868-69 on Ancestry.com.

Details on Moses Whittier's life from https://lowelllandtrust.org/greenwayclassroom/history/WhittierMill.pdf.

Source for spelling of Lucindia's name from Find a Grave: www.findagrave.com/memorial/179285694/lucindia-whittier; findagrave.com/memorial /179285637 /moses-whittier. Details on the Whittier Mills in Lowell from the Lowell Land and Trust, https://lowelllandtrust.org/greenwayclassroom/history/WhittierMill.pdf.

Information on the Whittier Mills in Georgia from "History of the Whittier Mills in Georgia," https://georgiahistory.com/ghmi_marker_updated/whittier-cotton-mills-and-village/; Whittier Cotton Mills Records, 1897–1933 Atlanta History Center WorldCat record id: 642044480, https://snaccooperative.org/view/20086777; Riverwalk Atlanta, www.riverwalkatlanta.org/whittier/index.htm; Whittier Mill Village, www.whittiermillvillage.com/about-us.html; Whittier Mill Village, podcast by Victoria Lemos, https://www.archiveatlantapodcast.com/e/whittier-mill-village/; Atlanta Upper West Side, www.atlantasupperwestside.com/SiteWhittierMillHistory.html; the *Athens Banner*, January 10, 1896; Harvey Newman, "Cotton Expositions in Atlanta," New Georgia Encyclopedia, last modified August 21, 2020, www.georgiaencyclopedia.org/articles/history-archaeology/cotton-expositions-in-atlanta/.

Chapter 3

Information on Lowell: Charles Cowley, *A History of Lowell*, 2nd rev. ed. (Boston: Lee & Shepard, 1868). Also Concord River Greenway, https://lowelllandtrust.org/greenwayclassroom. Information on women's clubs from *From the Past to the Future*; Wikipedia, "Woman's Club Movement in

the United States," https://en.wikipedia.org/wiki/Woman%27s_club_
movement_in_the_United_States; *Boston Globe*, "Women's Club Education
Program," May 26, 1913; Jennie June Croly, *The History of the Women's Club
Movement in America* (New York: Henry G. Allen & Co., 1889). XV clubs
details from Encyclopedia of Arkansas, https://encyclopediaofarkansas.
net/entries/xv-club-4541/, and *Official Registry and Directory of Women's Clubs
in America,* edited by Helen M. Winslow, 1914, see https://play.google.com/
books/reader?id=uUkMAQAAMAAJ&pg=GBS.PP1&printsec=frontcover.
Helen A. Whittier also served as an editor on this directory.

Chapter 4

Historical details from the Boston Public Library nineteenth-century
newspapers collection, the *Boston Globe* and *Boston Daily Advertiser*, July
22, 1895; John Lochhead collection of historic newspaper articles 1930s
and 1940s; and Harbor Islands photographs, Digital Commonwealth
and Boston Public Library special collections and Nathaniel Bradstreet
Shurtleff, *A Topographical and Historical Description of Boston, 1871* (Boston,
Boston City Council, 1871). Details on recreational sailing in the harbor
from *A History of the Boston Yacht Club* (self-published, 1891); Paul E.
Shanabrook, *The Boston: A History of the Boston Yacht Club 1866–1979*
(Boston: Yacht Club, Boston, 1979). Details about the endangered status
of the Boston Harbor Islands from the National Trust for Historic
Preservation, https://savingplaces.org/stories.

Chapter 5

Information on the snapshot era of nineteenth-century photography
relied on the following: Brian Coe and Paul Gates, *The Snapshot Photograph*
(London: Ash & Grant, 1977); Colin Ford and Ken Steinorth, eds., *You Press
the Button We do the Rest* (London: Dirk Nishen Publishing/The National
Museum of Photography, Film and Television, 1988); Sarah Greenough
and Diane Waggoner, *The Art of the American Snapshot 1888–1978*
(Washington, D.C.: National Gallery of Art/Princeton University Press,
2007); Reese V. Jenkins, *Images and Enterprise: Technology and the American*

Photographic Industry, 1839–1925 (Baltimore: Johns Hopkins University Press, 1975); Beaumont Newhall, *The History of Photography* (Boston: New York Graphic Society/Museum of Modern Art, 1964); Proprietors of the Kodak Patents, *Catalogue of Kodaks* (Rochester, NY: Eastman Kodak Company, 1892); Maribeth Keene and Brad Quinn, "Who's That Kodak Girl? Early Camera Ads Depict Women as Adventurous Shutterbugs," *Collectors Weekly*, April 15, 2010, www.collectorsweekly.com; Clive Thompson, "The Invention of the Snapshot Changed the Way We Viewed the World," *Smithsonian Magazine*, September 2014, www.smithsonianmag.com; and Penobscot Marine Museum, "The Evolution of the Photographic Snapshot," https://penobscotmarinemuseum.org.

CHAPTER 6

July 15: Recipe for Rochester jelly cake, "How to Make Rochester Jelly-Cake," https://chestofbooks.com. Depending on the availability of gas or electricity, some people had gas or electric ovens, but the thermostat was not invented until early in the twentieth century. See A. Verbon, "The History of the Oven—A Timeline," foodcrumbles.com.

July 19: Information on catboats from John R. Stilgoe, *Alongshore, New Haven & London* (New Haven, CT: Yale University Press, 1994).

July 21: Sources on women's evolving fashions of the nineteenth century from Anne M. Buck, *Victorian Costume and Costume Accessories* (London: Herbert Jenkins, 1961); Joan E. DeJean, *The Essence of Style: How the French Invented High Fashion, Fine Food, Chic Cafes, Style, Sophistication, and Glamour* (London: Free Press, 2005); Lydia Lane, "The Changing Silhouette of Victorian Women's Fashions: 1890s," Hagen History Center, August 4, 2021, www.ErieHistory.org/blog.

July 25: Information on women's bathing suits from Fashion History Timetable, https://fashionhistory.fitnyc.edu and Wikipedia, https://en.wikipedia.org/wiki/Swimsuit#Pre-20th_century.

July 26: Sources include Hull Yacht Club, *Handbook for 1891*; *Unitarian Christian Journals: Yesterday and Today* at www.americanunitarian.org/journals.htm; *The Sacred Heart Review* 6, no. 13 (August 1891) at https://newspapers.bc.edu.

July 27: Sources include Bernice Selden, *The Mill Girls: Lucy Larcom, Harriet Hanson Robinson, Sarah G. Bagley* (New York: Atheneum, 1983).

CHAPTER 7

The memories of Great Brewster Islanders come from a special FBHI project. In 2008, FBHI gathered people who had once spent summers on Great Brewster Island on the island and videotaped their recollections. The result was: "1930s Island Voices—Living on Great Brewster." Other sources for this chapter are: *Exploring Great Brewster Island: A Self-Guided brochure*, Massachusetts Department of Conservation and Recreation; *Cultural Landscape Report: Boston Harbor Islands National and State Park Volume 2: Existing Conditions*, prepared by the Olmsted Center for Historic Preservation, National Park Service, Boston, MA 2000/2017.

INDEX

ABOUT THE AUTHORS

Many of our team are members of the Friends of the Boston Harbor Islands (FBHI).

ANN MARIE ALLEN joined FBHI in 2016 and is a member of its Board of Directors. She is a Certified Interpretive Host through the National Association for Interpretation and has enjoyed volunteering with Visitor Services on Spectacle Island.

ALLISON ANDREWS catalogues historical materials and is a longtime FBHI member who has volunteered, visited and sailed among the Boston Harbor Islands.

VIVIAN BOREK is an award-winning editor, classical music commentator and travel planner. She created an abridged, illustrated edition of her mother's diary detailing daily life during the 1930s and 1940s in Woonsocket, Rhode Island, then a major mill town along the Blackstone River. She presents travelogs on her many solo visits in France.

ELIZABETH CARELLA is a photographic historian and photographer for international preservation projects. She is a researcher on Rainsford Island and leads tours of that island for the FBHI.

CAROL FITHIAN has, over a span of thirty years, been a Boston Harbor Islands volunteer, park ranger, boat narrator, FBHI Coordinator of Volunteers, trainer and writer.

WALTER HOPE is Chair of the FBHI and has lived on a boat in Boston Harbor since 2004. Walter's introduction to the harbor was back in the mid-1980s when he worked with the FBHI as a volunteer and Island Captain on Grape Island. He is currently a branch chief with the Massachusetts Department of Environmental Protection.

PAM INDECK is a retired human resource director who has lived on Boston Harbor the majority of her life.

MARGUERITE KRUPP is a longtime volunteer with the Friends of the Boston Harbor Islands, including two summers volunteering on Great Brewster. Her specialties include island birds and other critters, plants, history and teaching people how to make a whistle out of a periwinkle shell. Marguerite is a writer, editor, teacher, photographer and a great storyteller.

SUZANNE GALL MARSH is the FBHI Founder, current Board member and Coordinator of the Island Voices projects. She was a National Park ranger for the Boston Harbor Islands and a Gallops Island seasonal resident interpreter.

MARTHA MAYO is the retired director of the Center for Lowell History University of Massachusetts–Lowell, and author and/or consultant on many books, articles and exhibits on Lowell history.

STEPHANIE SCHOROW, Great Brewster journal project coordinator, is the author of eight books about Boston history, including *East of Boston: Notes from the Harbor Islands* and *The Cocoanut Grove Nightclub: A Boston Tragedy*, both for The History Press. She fell in love with the Boston Harbor Islands at first glance in 1994.